THE BEST GUITAR CHORD SONG BOOK EVER

PARTS 1-4

OMNIBUS PRESS

Order No. OP48141
ISBN: 0-7119-7663-5

Book and cover design by Chloë Alexander
Photographs courtesy of London Features International

Exclusive Distributors
Book Sales Limited
8/9 Frith Street
London WIV 5TZ, UK

The Five Mile Press
22 Summit Road
Noble Park
Victoria 3174, Australia

To the Music Trade only:
Music Sales Limited
8/9 Frith Street
London W1V 5TZ, UK

Printed by Caligraving Ltd, Norfolk

Visit Omnibus Press on the web at www.omnibuspress.com

THE BEST GUITAR CHORD
SONGBOOK EVER!

CONTENTS

Relative Tuning

The guitar can be tuned with the aid of pitch pipes or dedicated electronic guitar tuners which are available through your local music dealer. If you do not have a tuning device, you can use relative tuning. Estimate the pitch of the 6th string as near as possible to E or at least a comfortable pitch (not too high, as you might break other strings in tuning up). Then, while checking the various positions on the diagram, place a finger from your left hand on the:

5th fret of the E or 6th string and **tune the open A** (or 5th string) to the note (A)

5th fret of the A or 5th string and **tune the open D** (or 4th string) to the note (D)

5th fret of the D or 4th string and **tune the open G** (or 3rd string) to the note (G)

4th fret of the G or 3rd string and **tune the open B** (or 2nd string) to the note (B)

5th fret of the B or 2nd string and **tune the open E** (or 1st string) to the note (E)

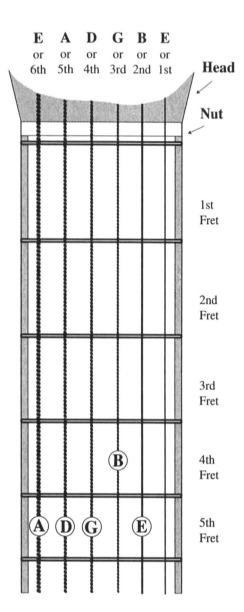

Reading Chord Boxes

Chord boxes are diagrams of the guitar neck viewed head upwards, face on as illustrated. The top horizontal line is the nut, unless a higher fret number is indicated, the others are the frets.

The vertical lines are the strings, starting from E (or 6th) on the left to E (or 1st) on the right.

The black dots indicate where to place your fingers.

Strings marked with an O are played open, not fretted.

Strings marked with an X should not be played.

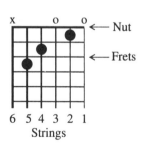

D'YOU KNOW WHAT I MEAN?

Words & Music by Noel Gallagher

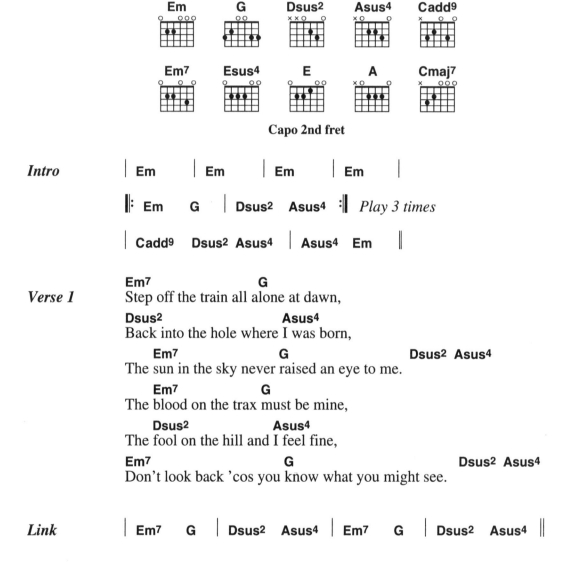

Capo 2nd fret

Intro | Em | Em | Em | Em |

‖: Em   G | Dsus2   Asus4 :‖ *Play 3 times*

| Cadd9   Dsus2 Asus4 | Asus4   Em ‖

Verse 1

Em7   G
Step off the train all alone at dawn,

Dsus2   Asus4
Back into the hole where I was born,

   Em7   G   Dsus2 Asus4
The sun in the sky never raised an eye to me.

   Em7   G
The blood on the trax must be mine,

   Dsus2   Asus4
The fool on the hill and I feel fine,

Em7   G   Dsus2 Asus4
Don't look back 'cos you know what you might see.

Link | Em7   G | Dsus2 Asus4 | Em7   G | Dsus2 Asus4 ‖

Verse 2

Em7   G
Look into the wall of my minds eye,

Dsus2   Asus4
I think I know but I don't know why

  Em7   G   Dsus2 Asus4
The questions are the answers you might need.

Em7   G
Coming in a mess going out in style,

 Dsus2   Asus4
I ain't good looking but I'm someone's child,

Em7   G   Dsus2 Asus4
No-one can give me the air that's mine to breathe.

Bridge 1

  Esus4 E   Dsus2 A
I met my maker, I made him cry,

   Esus4 E   Dsus2 A
And on my shoulder he asked me why,

   Esus4 E   Dsus2 A
His people won't fly through the storm,

    Cmaj7   Dsus2   A
I said, "Listen up man, they don't even know you're born".

Chorus 1

Em   G   Dsus2
All my people right here, right now,

A   Em G   Dsus2 A
 D'you know what I mean? _____ Yeah, yeah.

Em   G   Dsus2
All my people right here, right now,

A   Em G   Dsus2 A
 D'you know what I mean? _____ Yeah, yeah.

Em   G   Dsus2
All my people right here, right now,

A   Em G   Dsus2 A
 D'you know what I mean? _____ Yeah, yeah.

    Em G Dsus2 A
Yeah, yeah,

    Em G Dsus2 A
Yeah, yeah.

Verse 3

Em⁷   G
I don't really care for what you believe,
      Dsus²   Asus⁴
So open up your fist or you won't receive
      Em⁷   G   Dsus² Asus⁴
The thoughts and the words of every man you'll need.
      Em⁷   G
So get up off the floor and believe in life,
      Dsus²   Asus⁴
No-one's ever gonna ever ask you twice,
Em⁷   G   Dsus² Asus⁴
Get on the bus and bring it on home to me.

Bridge 2

      Esus⁴ E   Dsus²   A
I met my maker, I made him cry,
      Esus⁴ E   Dsus² A
And on my shoulder he asked me why,
     Esus⁴ E   Dsus²   A
His people won't fly through the storm,
      Cmaj⁷   Dsus²   A
I said, "Listen up man, they don't even know you're born".

Chorus 2

Em   G   Dsus²
All my people right here, right now,
A   Em G   Dsus² A
  D'you know what I mean? _____   Yeah, yeah.
Em   G   Dsus²
All my people right here, right now,
A   Em G   Dsus² A
  D'you know what I mean? _____   Yeah, yeah.
Em   G   Dsus²
All my people right here, right now,
A   Em G   Dsus² A
  D'you know what I mean?   Yeah, yeah,   yeah,
Em   G   Dsus² A   ————
Yeah,   yeah,
Em   G   Dsus² A
Yeah,   yeah,
Em   G   Dsus² A
Yeah,   yeah.

Middle |: Cmaj⁷ Dsus² Cmaj⁷ | Cmaj⁷ Dsus² Cmaj⁷ |

| Cmaj⁷ Dsus² Asus⁴ | Asus⁴ | Asus⁴ ‖

Solo ‖: Em G | Dsus² Asus⁴ | Em G | Dsus² Asus⁴ :‖

Chorus 3

Em   G   Dsus²
All my people right here, right now,

A   Em G   Dsus² A
  D'you know what I mean? _____   Yeah, yeah.

Em   G   Dsus²
All my people right here, right now,

A   Em G   Dsus² A
  D'you know what I mean? _____   Yeah, yeah.

Em   G   Dsus²
All my people right here, right now,

A   Em G   Dsus² A
  D'you know what I mean? _____   Yeah, yeah.

         Em   G   Dsus² A
Yeah, yeah,   yeah, yeah,

         Em   G   Dsus² A
Yeah, yeah,   yeah, yeah.

Outro | Cmaj⁷ Dsus² Cmaj⁷ | Cmaj⁷ Dsus² Cmaj⁷ |

| Cmaj⁷ Dsus² Em ‖

STAND BY ME

Words & Music by Noel Gallagher

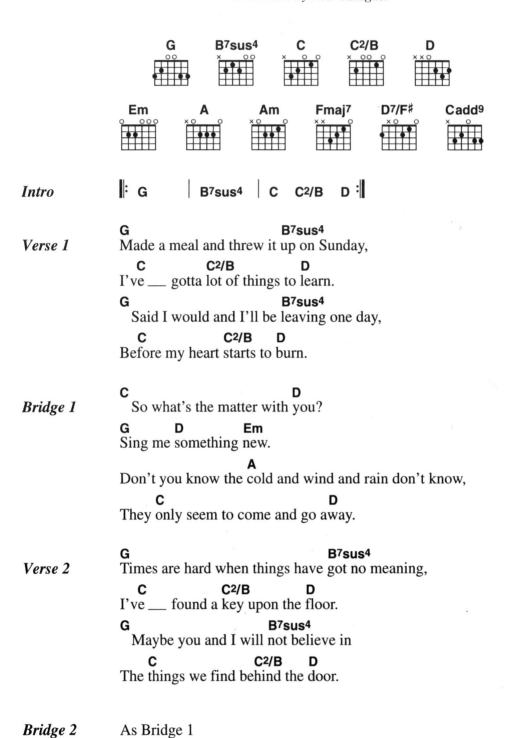

Intro ‖: G | B⁷sus⁴ | C C2/B D :‖

Verse 1

G   B⁷sus⁴
Made a meal and threw it up on Sunday,
    C   C2/B   D
I've __ gotta lot of things to learn.
G   B⁷sus⁴
  Said I would and I'll be leaving one day,
    C   C2/B   D
Before my heart starts to burn.

Bridge 1

    C   D
  So what's the matter with you?
G   D   Em
Sing me something new.
                          A
Don't you know the cold and wind and rain don't know,
        C   D
They only seem to come and go away.

Verse 2

G   B⁷sus⁴
Times are hard when things have got no meaning,
    C   C2/B   D
I've __ found a key upon the floor.
G   B⁷sus⁴
  Maybe you and I will not believe in
    C   C2/B   D
The things we find behind the door.

Bridge 2   As Bridge 1

Chorus 1

G   D   Am
   Stand by me, nobody knows, ____

             C   Fmaj7   D7/F♯
The way it's gonna be.

G   D   Am
   Stand by me, nobody knows, ____

             C   Fmaj7   D7/F♯
The way it's gonna be.

G   D   Am
   Stand by me, nobody knows, ____

             C   Fmaj7   D7/F♯
The way it's gonna be.

G   D   Am
   Stand by me, nobody knows, ____

         C
Yeah, nobody knows, ____

D   G
   The way it's gonna be.

Verse 3

G   B7sus4
   If you're leaving, will you take me with you?

     C   C2/B   D
I'm tired of talking on my phone.

G   B7sus4
There is one thing I can never give you,

     C   C2/B   D
My heart can never be your home.

Bridge 3

    C   D
   So what's the matter with you?

G   D   Em
Sing me something new.

             A
Don't you know the cold and wind and rain don't know,

     C   D
They only seem to come and go away.

    G   D   Am
Stand by me, nobody knows, ____

               C Fmaj7 D7/F#
The way it's gonna be.

    G   D   Am
Stand by me, nobody knows, ____

               C Fmaj7 D7/F#
The way it's gonna be.

    G   D   Am
Stand by me, nobody knows, ____

               C Fmaj7 D7/F#
The way it's gonna be.

    G   D   Am
Stand by me, nobody knows, ____

            C
Yeah, nobody knows, ____

D   Em D Cadd9
The way it's gonna be.

Cadd9   Em   D Cadd9
The way it's gonna be, yeah,

Cadd9   Em   D7/F# Cadd9
Maybe I can see, yeah.

Cadd9   A
Don't you know the cold and wind and rain don't know,

    C   D
They only seem to come and go away. Hey!

Chorus 4

    G   D   Am
Stand by me, nobody knows, ____

               C Fmaj7 D7/F#
The way it's gonna be.

    G   D   Am
Stand by me, nobody knows, ____

               C Fmaj7 D7/F#
The way it's gonna be.

    G   D   Am
Stand by me, nobody knows, ____

               C Fmaj7 D7/F#
The way it's gonna be.

    G   D   Am
Stand by me, nobody knows, ____

            C
Yeah, God only knows, ____

D   G
The way it's gonna be.

SUPERSONIC

Words & Music by Noel Gallagher

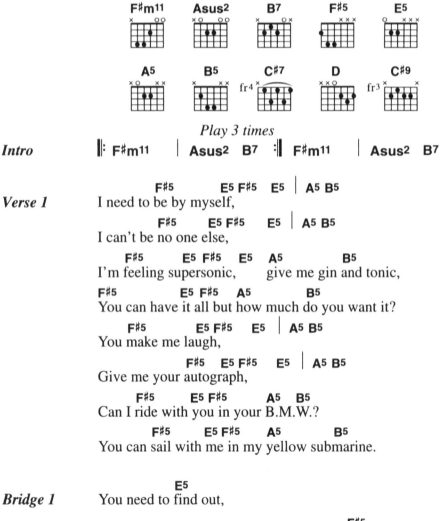

Play 3 times

Intro ‖: F#m11 | Asus2 B7 :‖ F#m11 | Asus2 B7

Verse 1
    F#5   E5 F#5 E5 | A5 B5
I need to be by myself,

     F#5 E5 F#5 E5 | A5 B5
I can't be no one else,

    F#5 E5 F#5 E5 A5   B5
I'm feeling supersonic, give me gin and tonic,

F#5   E5 F#5 A5   B5
You can have it all but how much do you want it?

   F#5   E5 F#5 E5 | A5 B5
You make me laugh,

     F#5 E5 F#5 E5 | A5 B5
Give me your autograph,

  F#5   E5 F#5 A5 B5
Can I ride with you in your B.M.W.?

     F#5 E5 F#5 A5   B5
You can sail with me in my yellow submarine.

Bridge 1
     E5
You need to find out,

                 F#5
'Cause no one's gonna tell you what I'm on about.

     E5
You need to find a way,

          C#7
For what you want to say, but before tomorrow.

	D A5 E5 F#5
Chorus 1	'Cause my friend said he'd take you home,

Chorus 1

       D   A5   E5   F#5
'Cause my friend said he'd take you home,

         D   A5   E5   F#5
He sits in a corner all alone.

D   A5   E5   F#5
He lives under a waterfall,

D   A5
Nobody can see him,

E5   F#5   D   A5
Nobody can ever hear him call,

E5   F#5   D   A5
Nobody can ever hear him call.

Guitar solo | E5 F#5 | D   A5 | E5 F#5 | D   A5 |

                   | E5 F#5 | E5 | E5 | C#9 | C#9

                           F#5   E5 F#5   E5 | A5 B5
Verse 2   You need to be yourself,

                    F#5   E5 F#5   E5 | A5 B5
You can't be no one else.

    F#5   E5   F#5 E5   A5   B5
I know a girl called Elsa, she's into Alka Seltzer,

      F#5   E5 F#5   A5   B5
She sniffs it through a cane on a supersonic train.

         F#5   E5 F#5 E5 | A5 B5
And she makes me laugh,

         F#5   E5 F#5   E5 | A5 B5
I got her autograph.

        F#5   E5 F#5   E5 A5   B5
She's done it with a doctor   on a helicopter,

       F#5   E5 F#5   E5 A5   B5
She's sniffin' in her tissue, sellin' the big issue.

               E5
Bridge 2   When she finds out,

                                 F#5
'Cause no ones's gonna tell her what I'm on about.

              E5
You need to find a way

                    C#7
For what you want to say, but before tomorrow.

Continued on next page...

Chorus 2

       D   **A5**   **E5**   **F#5**
'Cause my friend said he'd take you home,

    D   **A5**   **E5** **F#5**
He sits in a corner all alone.

D   **A5**   **E5** **F#5**
He lives under a waterfall,

D   **A5**
Nobody can see him,

E5   **F#5**   **D**   **A5**
Nobody can ever hear him call,

E5   **F#5**   **D**   **A5**
Nobody can ever hear him call.

Guitar solo   ‖: **E5** **F#5** │ **D**   **A5** :‖   *Repeat to fade*

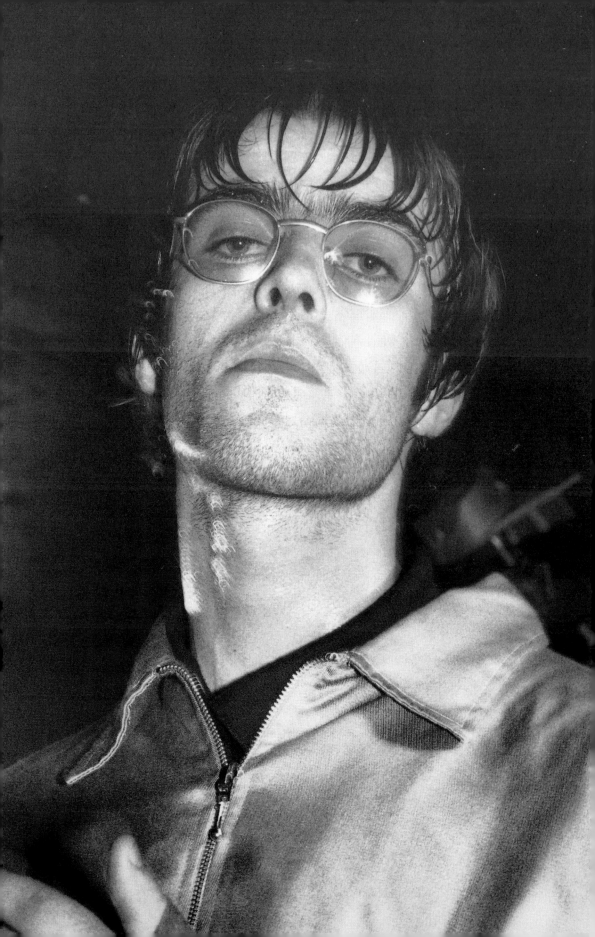

LINGER

Words by Dolores O'Riordan. Music by Dolores O'Riordan & Noel Hogan

Dadd⁴ D A⁶ A C Cmaj⁷ G

Intro

‖: Dadd⁴ | D | Dadd⁴ | D :‖ Dadd⁴ ‖

| A⁶ A | A⁶ | C Cmaj⁷ | C Cmaj⁷ | G | G ‖

Verse 1

   D
If you, if you could return,
       A⁶
Don't let it burn, don't let it fade.
          C
I'm sure I'm not being rude,

But it's just your attitude,
       G
It's tearing me apart,

It's ruining ev'rything.

Verse 2

   D
I swore, I swore I would be true,
        A⁶
And honey, so did you,
           C
So why were you holding her hand?

Is that the way we stand?
        G
Were you lying all the time?

Was it just a game to you?

                                        D
Chorus 1   But I'm in so deep,

                              A6
              You know I'm such a fool for you,

                                          C   **Cmaj7**
              You got me wrapped around your finger, ah, ah, ha.
              C   **G**
                Do you have to let it linger?

              Do you have to, do you have to,
                                    D
              Do you have to let it linger?

                              A6
Middle   Oh, I thought the world of you,

                              C   **Cmaj7**   **C**
              I thought nothing could go wrong,
              Cmaj7   **G**
              But I was wrong, I was wrong.

                            D
Verse 3   If you, if you could get by
                            A6
              Trying not to lie,

                                        C
              Things wouldn't get so confused,

              And I wouldn't feel so used,

                                    G
              But you always really knew

              I just wanna be with you.

                            D
Chorus 2   But I'm in so deep,

                              A6
              You know I'm such a fool for you,

                                          C   **Cmaj7**
              You got me wrapped around your finger, ah, ah, ha.
              C   **G**
                Do you have to let it linger?

              Do you have to, do you have to,
                                    D
              Do you have to let it linger?

Solo | **D** | **D** | **A6** | **A6** | **C Cmaj7** | **C Cmaj7** | **G** | **G**   ‖

                              D
Chorus 3   But I'm in so deep,
                                    A6
                You know I'm such a fool for you,
                                              C   **Cmaj7**
                You got me wrapped around your finger, ah, ah, ha.
                C   **G**
                  Do you have to let it linger?

                Do you have to, do you have to,
                                    D
                Do you have to let it linger?

                                    A6
Chorus 4   You know I'm such a fool for you,
                                              C   **Cmaj7**
                You got me wrapped around your finger, ah, ah, ha.
                C   **G**
                  Do you have to let it linger?

                Do you have to, do you have to,
                                    D
                Do you have to let it linger?

Instrumental | **D** | **D** | **A6** | **A6** | **C Cmaj7** | **C Cmaj7** | **G** | **G** |

                | **D** | **D Dadd4** | **D** | **D Dadd4** | **D** | **D Dadd4** | **D**   ‖

ZOMBIE

Words & music by Dolores O'Riordan

Em   Cmaj7   G6   G6/F#

Intro   ‖: Em | Cmaj7 | G6 | G6/F# :‖ *Play 4 times*

Verse 1

Em   Cmaj7
Another head hangs lowly,

G6   G6/F#
Child is slowly taken.

Em   Cmaj7
And the violence caused such silence,

G6   G6/F#
Who are we mistaken?

              Em
But you see, it's not me,

        Cmaj7
It's not my family,

        G6
In your head, in your head,

           G6/F#
They are fighting.

            Em
With their tanks and their bombs

        Cmaj7
And their bombs and their guns,

        G6   G6/F#
In your head, in your head they are crying.

Chorus 1

        Em   Cmaj7
In your head, in your head,

        G6   G6/F#
Zombie, zombie, zombie,   hey, hey.

              Em   Cmaj7
What's in your head, in your head?

        G6   G6/F#
Zombie, zombie, zombie,   hey, hey, hey.

Bridge 1

      Em   Cmaj⁷
Oh, doo, doo, doo, doo,

               G⁶
Doo, doo, doo, doo,

              G⁶/F♯
Doo, doo, doo, doo,

               Em Cmaj⁷ G⁶ G⁶/F♯
Doo, doo, doo, doo.

Verse 2

    Em   Cmaj⁷   G⁶
  Another mother's breakin' heart

          G⁶/F♯
Is taking over.

Em   Cmaj⁷
  When the violence causes silence,

G⁶   G⁶/F♯
We must be mistaken.

           Em
It's the same old theme

        Cmaj⁷
Since nine - teen sixteen,

    G⁶
In your head, in your head,

          G⁶/F♯
They're still fighting.

        Em
With their tanks and their bombs

      Cmaj⁷
And their bombs and their guns,

    G⁶   G⁶/F♯
In your head, in your head they are dying.

Chorus 2   As Chorus 1

Bridge 2

Em
Oh, oh, oh, oh,

Cmaj⁷
Oh, oh, oh, hey,

G⁶   G⁶/F♯
Oh, ya, ya.

Instrumental | Em | Cmaj⁷ | G⁶ | G⁶/F♯ ‖: Em | Cmaj⁷ | Em | Cmaj⁷ :‖

Solo   ‖: Em | Cmaj⁷ | G⁶ | G⁶/F♯ :‖ *Play 4 times*

       | Em | Cmaj⁷ | Em | Cmaj⁷ | Em | Cmaj⁷ | Em ‖

THE LONG AND WINDING ROAD

Words & Music by John Lennon & Paul McCartney

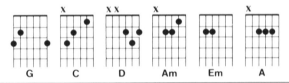

G   C   D   Am   Em   A

     Em   **D**
The long and winding road,
    G   **C**
That leads to your door,
    G   **Em**
Will never disappear,
Am   **D**   **G**
I've seen that road before.
C **G**   **Em**
It always leads me here,
Am   **D**   **G**
Lead me to your door.

     Em   **D**
The wild and windy night,
     G   **C**
That the rain washed away,
G   **Em**
Has left a pool of tears,
Am   **D**   **G**
Crying for the day.
C   **G**   **Am**
Why leave me standing here?
Am   **D**   **G**
Let me know the way.

G   **C**   **G**   **Am** **D**
Many times I've been alone and many times I've cried.
G   **C**   **G**   **Am**
Anyway you'll never know the many ways I've tried.

     Em   **D**
But still they lead me back,
     G   **C**
To the long winding road.
     G   **Em**
You left me standing here,
Am   **D**   **G**
A long long time ago.

C   **G**   **Em**
Don't leave me waiting here,
Am   **D**   **G**
Lead me to your door.
Am **D**   **G**
Yeh, yeh, yeh, yeh.

PAPERBACK WRITER

Words & Music by John Lennon & Paul McCartney

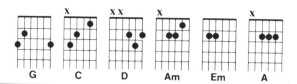

G C D Am Em A

G
Sir or madam will you read my book,

It took me years to write, will you take a look?

It's based on a novel by a man named Lear and I need a job,
          C
So I wanna be a paperback writer
    G
Paperback writer.

     G
It's the dirty story of a dirty man

And his clinging wife doesn't understand.

His son is working for the Daily Mail, it's a steady job
         C
But he wants to be a paperback writer,
    G **C**   **G**
Paperback writer, paperback writer.

     G
It's a thousand pages, give or take a few,

I'll be writing more in a week or two.

I can make it longer if you like the style I can change it round
          C
And I want to be a paperback writer,
    G
Paperback writer.

     G
If you really like it you can have the rights,

It could make a million for you overnight.

If you must return it you could send it here but I need a break
         C
And I want to be a paperback writer,
    G
Paperback writer,
C   **G**
Paperback writer . . . *Repeat 'till fade*

I FEEL FINE

Words & Music by John Lennon & Paul McCartney

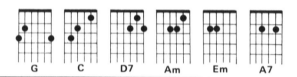

G   C   D7   Am   Em   A7

G
Baby's good to me, you know

She's happy as can be, you know
D7
She said so
       C   **G**
I'm in love with her and I feel fine.

G
Baby says she's mine, you know

She tells me all the time, you know
D7
She said so
       C   **G**
I'm in love with her and I feel fine.

G   **C**   **D7**
I'm so glad that she's my little girl
G   **C**   **D7**
She's so glad, she's telling all the world.

     G
That her baby buys her things, you know

He buys her diamond rings, you know
D7
She said so
      C   **G**
She's in love with me and I feel fine
D7   **C**   **G**
She's in love with me and I feel fine.

OUT OF THE SINKING

Words & Music by Paul Weller

Intro | E | E | Emaj7 | Emaj7 | Emaj7 | Emaj7 ||

Verse 1

E
Past midnight's hold,

F#m7/11
Where the world's awaiting,

E   Emaj7*
I'll wait for your love,

B6 B
     But I close my eyes,

A6 A   E
     As there's pain too in paradise,

And we pay our price.

Chorus 1

C#m7   F#m7/11
Hey baby say,   just what you're thinking,

C#m7   F#m7/11
Know I know it,   yeah, feel I'm sinking,

C#m7   F#m7/11
Know I feel it,   know you feel it too,

A5
Across the water,

There's a boat that will take us away.

Instrumental | Emaj7 | Emaj7 | Emaj7 | Emaj7 |
| D   A5   E | E | D   A5   E | E ||

Interlude

D   A5   E
It was shining for me,

D   A5   E
All I need it to be.

D   A5   E
But I can't find the key,

D   A5   B5
One to make me believe.

Instrumental | Emaj7 | Emaj7 | Emaj7 | Emaj7 ||

Solo | Emaj7 | Emaj7 | F#m7/11 | F#m7/11 | Emaj7 | Emaj7 ||

Verse 2

E
Late at night

F#m7/11
When the world is dreaming,

E   Emaj7*
Way past the stars

B6   B
That ignore our fate

A6   A   E
And all twinkle too late to save us,

So we save ourselves.

Chorus 2

C#m7   F#m7/11
Hey baby do   just what you're thinking,

C#m7   F#m7/11
Know I know it,   yeah, feel I'm sinking,

C#m7   F#m7/11
Know I feel it,   I know you feel it too,

A5
Across the water,

                          C#m7
There's a boat that will take us away.

C#m7   **F#m7/11**
Out of the sadness,   far from the madness,

C#m7   **F#m7/11**
Into sunlight,   yeah, out of the sinking,

C#m7   **F#m7/11**
Know I feel it, I know you feel it too

A5
Across the water,

There's a boat that will take us away,

Emaj7   **F#m/E**   **Emaj7 Gmaj7 A***
And there we'll stay.

| **Emaj7** | **Emaj7 Gmaj7 A*** | **Emaj7** | **Emaj7** |

| **D A5 E** | **E** | | **D A5 E** | **E** | ‖

D   **A5**   **E**
But I can't find the key.

| **D A5 E** | **E** ‖

STANLEY ROAD

Words & Music by Paul Weller

Gm   C/G   B♭m   E♭/B♭   E♭sus4/B♭   C   Cm   B♭m7

Am7   D9   D♭9   C9   D7$^{\#5}_{\#9}$ D   Am7*   F#m7

Intro

| Gm C/G | Gm C/G | Gm C/G | Gm C/G |

| B♭m E♭/B♭ | B♭m E♭/B♭ | B♭m E♭/B♭ | E♭sus4/B♭ E♭/B♭ |

| Gm C/G | Gm C/G | Gm C/G | Gm ‖

Verse 1

C
  A hazy mist hung down the street,
                            Cm   Gm   C/G Gm C/G Gm C/G Gm
The length of its mile as far as my eye could see.
C
  The sky so wide, the houses tall, or so they seemed to be,
               Cm   Gm   C/G Gm C/G Gm C/G Gm
So they seemed to be so small.

Chorus 1

         B♭m7
And it gleamed in the distance
Am7   D9 D♭9 C9   D7$^{\#5}_{\#9}$
  And it shone like the sun,   like silver and gold,
       Gm   C/G Gm C/G
It went on and on,
       Gm   C/G Gm C/G
It went on and on.

Verse 2

 C
  The summer nights that seemed so long
                     Cm   Gm   C/G Gm C/G Gm C/G Gm
Always call me back to return as I rewrite this song,   oh, yeah.
 C
  The ghosts of night, the dreams of day
                     Cm   Gm   C/G Gm C/G Gm C/G Gm
Make me swirl and fall and hold me in their sway.

       B♭m7   **Am7**   **D9**
And it's still in the distance and it shines like the sun,

D♭9 C9   **D7$^{\sharp5}_{\sharp9}$**   **Gm**   **C/G Gm C/G**
      Like silver and gold, it goes on and on.

         Gm   **C/G Gm C/G**
It goes on and on,

         Gm   **C/G Gm C/G**
It goes on and on,   yeah,

         Gm   **C/G Gm**
It goes on and on.

Middle 1

    D   **Am7***
  The rolling stock rocked me to sleep,

    D   **Am7***
  Amber lights flashing 'cross the street,

F♯m7   **Am7**   **C   D**
  And on the corner, a dream to meet,

         Gm   **C/G Gm C/G**
Yeah, going on and on.

Solo | **Gm C/G** | **Gm C/G** | **Gm C/G** | **Gm C/G** |

              | **B♭m E♭/B♭** | **B♭m E♭/B♭** | **B♭m E♭/B♭** | **E♭sus4/B♭ E♭/B♭** |

              | **Gm C/G** | **Gm C/G** | **Gm C/G** | **Gm** |

              | **B♭m7 E♭/B♭** | **B♭m7 E♭/B♭** | **Am7** | **D9** | **D♭9 C9** | **D7$^{\sharp5}_{\sharp9}$** | |

              | **Gm C/G** | **Gm C/G** | **Gm C/G** | **Gm C/G** ‖

Middle 2   As Middle 1

         Gm   **C/G Gm C/G**
Going on and on,

         Gm   **C/G Gm C/G**
It goes on and on,   yeah,

         Gm   **C/G** **Gm**   **C/G**
It goes on and on, yeah, on and on.

Solo | **Gm C/G** | **Gm C/G** | **Gm C/G** | **Gm** |

              ‖: **B♭m7 E♭/B♭** | **B♭m7 E♭/B♭** | **B♭m7 E♭/B♭** | **E♭sus4/B♭ E♭/B♭** :‖

                                       Repeat to fade

SHADOW OF THE SUN

Words & Music by Paul Weller

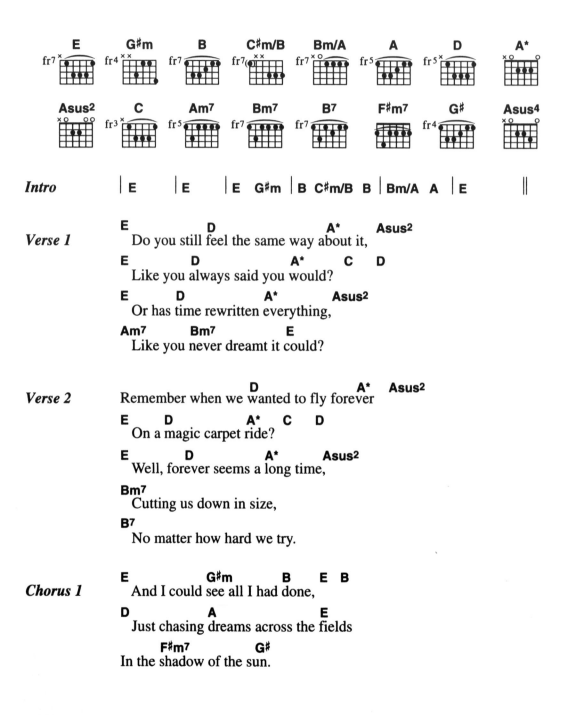

Intro | E | E | E G#m | B C#m/B B | Bm/A A | E   ‖

Verse 1
```
      E              D                A*    Asus²
      Do you still feel the same way about it,
      E         D              A*      C   D
      Like you always said you would?
      E         D              A*       Asus²
      Or has time rewritten everything,
      Am⁷      Bm⁷              E
      Like you never dreamt it could?
```

Verse 2
```
                       D               A*   Asus²
      Remember when we wanted to fly forever
      E       D              A*   C   D
      On a magic carpet ride?
      E         D              A*      Asus²
      Well, forever seems a long time,
      Bm⁷
      Cutting us down in size,
      B⁷
      No matter how hard we try.
```

Chorus 1
```
      E              G#m        B    E  B
      And I could see all I had done,
      D          A              E
      Just chasing dreams across the fields
            F#m⁷             G#
      In the shadow of the sun.
```

(cont)

    E   **G♯m**   **B**   **E B**
And I plan to have it all while I'm still young

    D   **A**   **E**
And chase the dreams across my fields,

        D   **A**
In the shadow of the sun,

    E   **D**   **C** **D**
Deep in the shadow of the sun.

‖ **E**   ‖ **C D E** ‖ **E** **C D** ‖

Verse 3

    E   **D**   **A***   **Asus2**
Once upon a time I might have told you,

    E   **D**   **A*** **C D**
But now nothing seems that plain.

    E   **D**   **A***   **Asus2**
However much we're changing

    Bm7
There are some things the same,

    B7
And those same things still say.

Chorus 2

    E   **G♯m**   **B**   **E B**
And I could see all I had done,

    D   **A**   **E**
Just chasing dreams across the fields

        F♯m7   **G♯**
In the shadow of the sun.

    E   **G♯m**   **B**   **E B**
And I plan to have it all while I'm still young

    D   **A**   **E**
And chase the fields across my dreams,

        D   **A**
In the shadow of the sun,

    E   **D**   **C** **D**
Deep in the shadow of the sun.

‖ **E**   ‖ **C D E** ‖ **E** **C D** ‖

Guitar solo ‖ **E** **D**   ‖ **A*** **Asus2** ‖ **E** **D**   ‖ **A*** **C D** ‖

                ‖ **E** **D**   ‖ **A*** **Asus2** ‖ **Am7** **Bm7** ‖ **E**   ‖

Verse 4

```
E                    D                  A*    Asus4  A*
Remember when we wanted to fly forever
E      D            A*    C  D
On a magic carpet ride?
E          D              A*        Asus2
Well, forever seems a long time,
Bm7
Cutting us down in size,
B7
No matter how hard we try.
```

Chorus 3   As Chorus 1

Outro

```
E      D            A
In the shadow of the sun,
E      D              C  D
In the shadow of the sun,
E          D            A
Oh, in the shadow of the sun,
E      D              C  D
In the shadow of the sun.
E                      C  D
In the shadow of the sun,
E                      C  D
In the shadow of the sun,
E
In the shadow of the sun.
```

                                              Repeat to fade

Instrumental ‖: C D C D | C D C D | C D C D | C D C D :‖

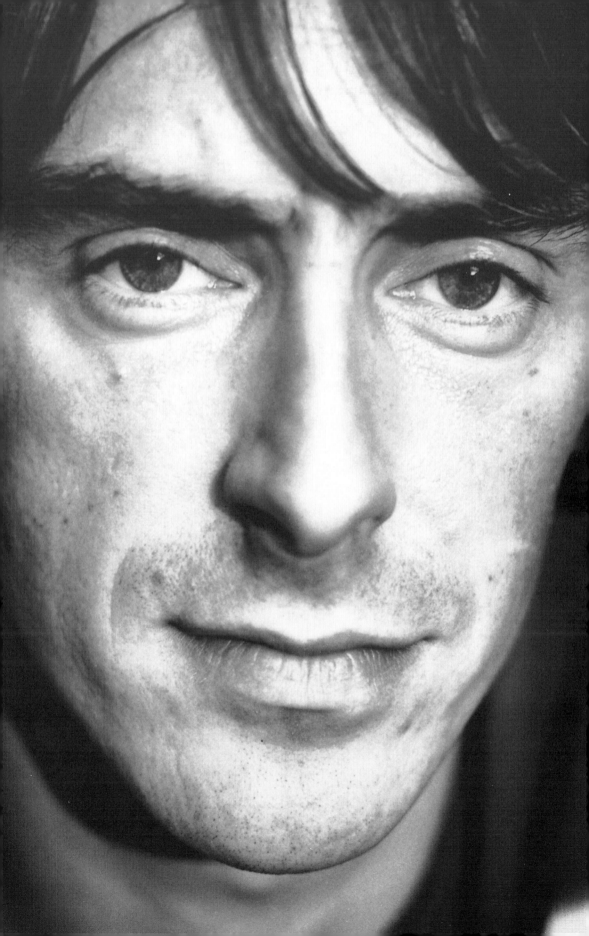

HEAD OVER FEET

Music by Alanis Morissette & Glenn Ballard. Lyrics by Alanis Morissette

C	G	Am	F	D	Bm	A	B♭	Asus⁴

Verse 1

  C G   Am   F   C
I had no choice but to hear you.

    G   Am   F   C
You stated your case time and again.

    G   Am   F
I thought about it.

Verse 2

   C   G   Am F   C
You treat me like I'm a princess.

    G   Am F   C
I'm not used to   liking that.

    G   Am   F
You ask how my day was.

Chorus 1

              D   Bm G   A
You've already won me over in spite of me.

              D   Bm B♭   Asus⁴
And don't be alarmed if I fall head over feet.

            D   Bm   G   A
Don't be surprised if I love you for all that you are,

F   C
I couldn't help it,

G
It's all your fault.

Verse 3

   C   G   Am F   C
Your love is thick and it swallowed me whole.

    G   Am   F   C
You're so much braver than I gave you credit for.

    G   Am   F
That's not lip service.

Chorus 2   As Chorus 1

Verse 4

```
C       G         Am   F               C
   You are the bearer of unconditional things.
     G           Am  F              C
You held your breath    and the door for me.
       G          Am    F
Thanks for your patience.
```

Solo   Chords as Chorus 1

Verse 5

```
C        G      Am          F            C
   You're the best listener that I've ever met.
       G              Am
You're my best friend,
F                      C
Best friend with benefits.
       G        Am     F
What took me so long.
```

Verse 6

```
C     G       Am   F                C
   I've never felt     this healthy before.
     G       Am  F                  C
I've never wanted     something rational.
  G   Am           F
I am aware now,
C     G   Am        F
   I am aware now.
```

Chorus 2   ‖: As Chorus 1 :‖   *Repeat to fade*

FORGIVEN

Music by Alanis Morissette & Glenn Ballard. Lyrics by Alanis Morissette

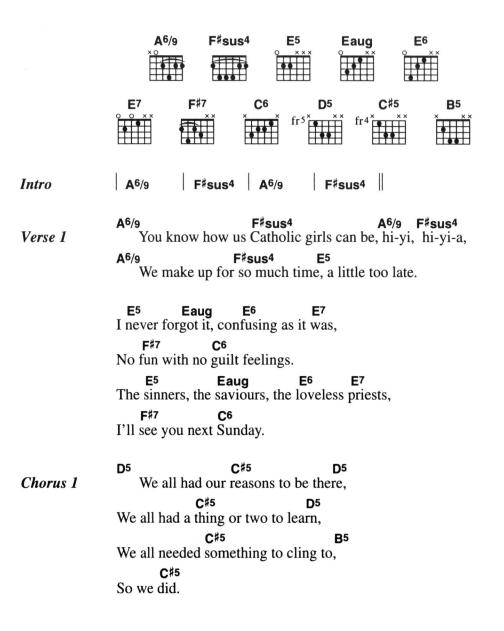

Intro | A6/9 | F#sus4 | A6/9 | F#sus4 ‖

Verse 1

A6/9   F#sus4   A6/9   F#sus4
   You know how us Catholic girls can be, hi-yi, hi-yi-a,

A6/9   F#sus4   E5
   We make up for so much time, a little too late.

E5   Eaug   E6   E7
I never forgot it, confusing as it was,

  F#7   C6
No fun with no guilt feelings.

E5   Eaug   E6   E7
The sinners, the saviours, the loveless priests,

  F#7   C6
I'll see you next Sunday.

Chorus 1

D5   C#5   D5
   We all had our reasons to be there,

    C#5   D5
We all had a thing or two to learn,

    C#5   B5
We all needed something to cling to,

   C#5
So we did.

Verse 2

A6/9   F#sus4   A6/9   F#sus4
I sang Alleluia in the choir, oh, Alleluia-luia-luia,
A6/9   F#sus4   E5
I confessed my darkest deeds to an envious man.

      E5   Eaug   E6   E7
My brothers they never went blind for what they did
     F#7   C6
But I may as well have.
      E5   Eaug   E6   E7
In the name of the Father, the Sceptic and the Son,
   F#7   C6
I had one more stupid question.

Chorus 2   As Chorus 1

Bridge   D5   E5   D5
           What I had learned I rejected, but I believed again,
                C#5   D5
I will suffer the consequence of this inquisition,
               E5   F#sus4 F#7
If I jump into this fountain, will I be forgiven?

Chorus 3   As Chorus 1

Outro chorus   D5   C#5   D5
          We all had delusions in our head,
             C#5   D5
We all had our minds made up for us,
           C#5   B5
We had to believe in something,
       C#5
So we did.
   D5   C#5   D5
     We all had our reasons to be there,
           C#5   D5
We all had a thing or two to learn,
           C#5   B5
We all needed something to cling to,
         C#5   D5   C#5
So we did.
         D5   C#5   D5
So we did.
      C#5   B5
Oo, ho, la, la, la, la,
       C#5 D5
So we did.

WAKE UP

Music by Alanis Morissette & Glenn Ballard. Lyrics by Alanis Morissette

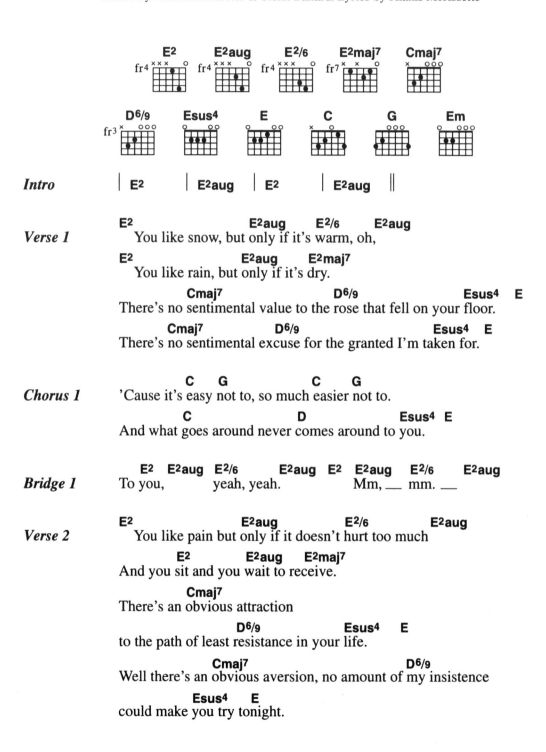

Intro | E2 | E2aug | E2 | E2aug ||

Verse 1

E2   E2aug   E2/6   E2aug
   You like snow, but only if it's warm, oh,

E2   E2aug   E2maj7
  You like rain, but only if it's dry.

      Cmaj7   D6/9   Esus4   E
There's no sentimental value to the rose that fell on your floor.

     Cmaj7   D6/9   Esus4   E
There's no sentimental excuse for the granted I'm taken for.

Chorus 1

      C   G   C   G
'Cause it's easy not to, so much easier not to.

     C   D   Esus4 E
And what goes around never comes around to you.

Bridge 1

    E2 E2aug E2/6   E2aug E2 E2aug   E2/6   E2aug
To you,   yeah, yeah.   Mm, __ mm. __

Verse 2

E2   E2aug   E2/6   E2aug
   You like pain but only if it doesn't hurt too much

     E2   E2aug   E2maj7
And you sit and you wait to receive.

     Cmaj7
There's an obvious attraction

        D6/9   Esus4   E
to the path of least resistance in your life.

     Cmaj7   D6/9
Well there's an obvious aversion, no amount of my insistence

     Esus4   E
could make you try tonight.

          C   **G**
'Cause it's easy not to,
           C   **G**
So much easier not to.
        C   **D**   **Esus4**   **E**
And what goes around never comes around to you.

    Cmaj7 D6/9   **Esus4 E**   **Cmaj7 D6/9** **Esus4 E**   **Em**
To you, —   to you, —   to you, —   to you, —   to you.

E2 E2aug E2/6 E2aug   **E2**
         Ooh, ooh,   there's no love,
   E2aug   **E2maj7**
no money, no thrill anymore.
          Cmaj7   **D6/9**
Well there's an apprehensive naked little trembling boy
            Esus4   **E**
With his head in his hands.
          Cmaj7   **D6/9**
And there's an underestimated and impatient little girl
         Esus4   **E**
Raising her hand.

         C   **G**
But it's easy not to,
         C   **G**
So much easier not to.
        C   **D**   **Esus4 E**
And what goes around never comes around to you.

    Cmaj7 D6/9   **Esus4 E**
To you, —   to you.
      Cmaj7 D6/9   **Esus4 E**   **Esus4 E**
Get up, get up, get up, off of it.
       Cmaj7 D6/9   **Esus4 E**   **Esus4 E**
Get up, get up, get up, off of it.
       Cmaj7 D6/9   **Esus4 E**   **Esus4 E**
Get out, get out of here, enough already.
      Cmaj7 D6/9   **Esus4 E**   **Esus4 E**
Get up, get up, get up, off of it.
N.C.
'N' wake up.

DISCO 2000

Music by Pulp. Lyrics by Jarvis Cocker

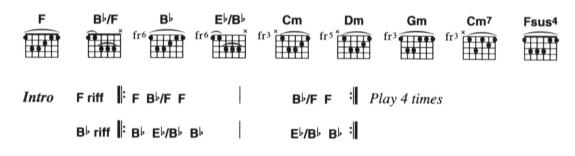

Intro   F riff ‖: F B♭/F F | B♭/F F :‖ *Play 4 times*

B♭ riff ‖: B♭ E♭/B♭ B♭ | E♭/B♭ B♭ :‖

Verse 1

                  F riff
Oh, we were born within an hour of each other,

Our mothers said we could be sister and brother,

          B♭ riff
Your name is De-bo-rah, Deborah,

It never suited ya.

       F riff
And they said that when we grew up,

We'd get married and never split up,

       B♭ riff
Oh, we never did it,

Although I often thought of it.

Pre-chorus 1

                   Cm
Oh, Deborah, do you recall?

Your house was very small,

With woodchip on the wall,

When I came round to call

             F
You didn't notice me at all.

Chorus 1

B♭
And I said "Let's all meet up in the year two thousand,

Dm   **Gm**
Won't it be strange when we're all fully grown,

                          Cm7   **Fsus4** **F**
Be there two o'clock by the fountain down the road."_____

B♭
I never knew that you'd get married,

Dm   **Gm**
I would be living down here on my own,

                       Cm7   **Fsus4** **F**
On that damp and lonely Thursday years ago. _____

Verse 2

F riff
You were the first girl at school to get breasts,

And Martyn said that you were the best,

        B♭ riff
Oh, the boys all loved you but I was a mess,

I had to watch them trying to get you undressed.

        F riff
We were friends, ____ that was how it went,

I used to walk you home sometimes but it meant,

        B♭ riff
Oh, it meant nothing to you

'Cause you were so popular.

Pre-chorus 2 As Pre-chorus 1

Chorus 2   As Chorus 1

Instrumental ‖: F B♭/F F | B♭/F F :‖

                ‖: B♭ E♭/B♭ B♭ | E♭/B♭ B♭ :‖

Pre-chorus 3
      Cm
Oh, Deborah, do you recall?

Your house was very small,

With woodchip on the wall,

When I came round to call
      F
You didn't notice me at all.

Chorus 3
      B♭
And I said "Let's all meet up in the year two thousand,
Dm   **Gm**
Won't it be strange when we're all fully grown,
              Cm⁷   **Fsus⁴** **F**
Be there two o'clock by the fountain down the road."_____
B♭
I never knew that you'd get married,
Dm   **Gm**
I would be living down here on my own,
              Cm⁷   **Fsus⁴** **F**
On that damp and lonely Thursday years ago. _____

Outro
B♭
What are you doin' Sunday, baby?
Dm
Would you like to come and meet me, maybe?
Gm   **Cm⁷** **Fsus⁴** **F**
You can even bring your baby, ooh. _____
B♭
What are you doin' Sunday, baby?
Dm
Would you like to come and meet me, maybe?
Gm   **Cm⁷** **Fsus⁴**   **F**   **B♭**
You can even bring your baby, ooh, _____ ooh. _____

SOMETHING CHANGED

Music by Pulp. Lyrics by Jarvis Cocker

G   Gsus4   G2   Bm   C   D   E   Am7   Dsus4

Intro   ‖: G   Gsus4 G   G2 | G   Gsus4 G   :‖

Verse 1

     G   Bm   C
  I wrote this song two hours before we met,

     G   Bm   C
  I didn't know your name or what you looked like yet.

              D   Bm   E
I could have stayed at home and gone to bed,

C   D   Bm   E
  I could have gone to see a film instead.

Bm   E   Am7   D
  You might have changed your mind and seen your friends,

Bm E   Am7   D
  Life could have been very diff'rent but then

Am7   D   Dsus4 D
  Something changed.

‖: G   Gsus4 G   G2 | G   Gsus4 G   :‖

Verse 2

                       Bm   C
Do you believe that there's someone up above?

     G   Bm   C
  And does he have a timetable directing acts of love?

              D   Bm   E
Why did I write this song on that one day?

C   D   Bm   E
  Why did you touch my hand and softly say

Bm   E   Am7 D
  "Stop asking questions that don't matter any - way,

Bm   E   Am7   D
  Just give us a kiss to celebrate here today."

Am7   D   Dsus4 D
  Something changed.

| G   Gsus⁴ G   G² | G   Gsus⁴ G   ‖

Instrumental ‖: G | G | Bm | C   :‖

Verse 3

           C   D
When we woke up that morning

      Bm   E
We had no way of knowing,

        C   D
That in a matter of hours

      Bm   E
We'd change the way we were going,

Bm   E
  Where would I be now?

Bm   E
  Where would I be now

      Am⁷ D
If we'd never met?

Bm   E
  Would I be singing this song

    Am⁷   D
To someone else instead?

      Am⁷   D   Dsus⁴ D
I don't know, but like you just said,

G
  Something changed.

SORTED FOR E'S AND WIZZ

Music by Pulp. Lyrics by Jarvis Cocker

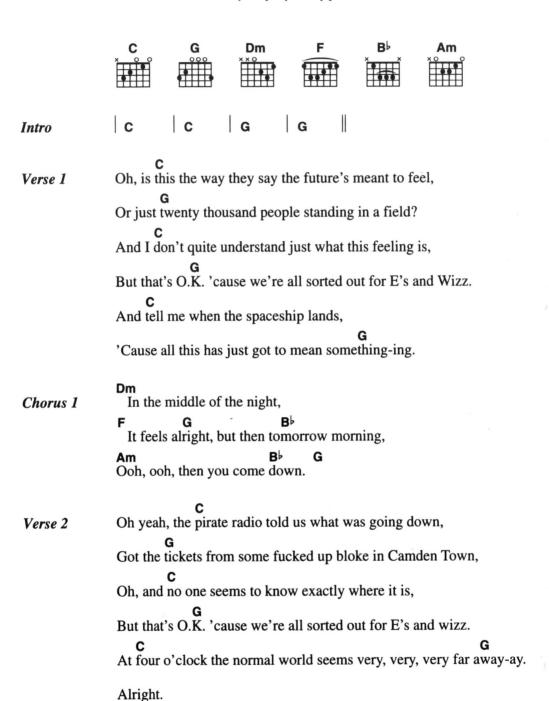

Intro | C | C | G | G   ‖

Verse 1

>   **C**
> Oh, is this the way they say the future's meant to feel,
>
>   **G**
> Or just twenty thousand people standing in a field?
>
>   **C**
> And I don't quite understand just what this feeling is,
>
>   **G**
> But that's O.K. 'cause we're all sorted out for E's and Wizz.
>
>   **C**
> And tell me when the spaceship lands,
>
>   **G**
> 'Cause all this has just got to mean something-ing.

Chorus 1

> **Dm**
>   In the middle of the night,
>
> **F**   **G**   **B♭**
>   It feels alright, but then tomorrow morning,
>
> **Am**   **B♭** **G**
> Ooh, ooh, then you come down.

Verse 2

>   **C**
> Oh yeah, the pirate radio told us what was going down,
>
>   **G**
> Got the tickets from some fucked up bloke in Camden Town,
>
>   **C**
> Oh, and no one seems to know exactly where it is,
>
>   **G**
> But that's O.K. 'cause we're all sorted out for E's and wizz.
>
>   **C**   **G**
> At four o'clock the normal world seems very, very, very far away-ay.
>
> Alright.

Chorus 2   As Chorus 1

                             C   **G**

Verse 3   Just keep on moving.

C
Everybody asks your name, they say we're all the same,

                 G
And now it's "Nice-one, geezer,"

But that's as far as conversation went.

   C
I lost my friends, I dance alone, it's six o'clock, I wanna go home,

G
  It's "No way," "Not today," makes you wonder what it meant.

C
  And this feeling grows,

And grows and grows and grows,

             G
And you want to call your mother and say,

"Mother, can I never come home again

C
  'Cause I seem to have left an important part of my brain somewhere,

G
  Somewhere in a field in Hampshire."

Alright.

         Dm

Chorus 3   In the middle of the night,

F   **G**   **B♭.**
  It feels alright, but then tomorrow morning,

Am   **B♭**
Ooh, ooh, then you come down.

Am   **B♭**
Ooh, ooh, then you come down.

Am   **B♭**
Ooh, what if you never come down?

THE BEST GUITAR CHORD SONGBOOK EVER!

CONTENTS

BAD MEDICINE

Words & Music by Jon Bon Jovi, Richie Sambora & Desmond Child

E   A   G   B   E5   F#5   D   G5

Chorus 1

    E   A E
Your love is like bad medicine,

A   E
Bad medicine is what I need,

                    A E
Oh, shake it up, just like bad medicine,

A   E
There ain't no doctor that can cure my disease.

Guitar riff | E | E A G | E | N.C Bad medicine.

Verse 1

E   A
I ain't got a fever, got a permanent disease,

        G E   A   G
And it'll take more than a doctor to prescribe a remedy,

  A
I got lots of money but it isn't what I need,

G   E   A   G
Gonna take more than a shot to get this poison out of me,

    B
And I got all the symptoms count 'em 1, 2, 3.

        E5
First you need (that's what you get for falling in love),

        E5
Then you bleed,

               F#5
And when you're on your knees (that's what you get for falling in love),

D   B
Now this boy's addicted, 'cause your kiss is the drug.

Chorus 2   As Chorus 1

G   A E
Bad, bad medicine.

Verse 2
```
E                                        A
I don't need no needle to be giving me a thrill,
      G    E                                    A
And I don't need no anaesthesia or a nurse to bring a pill,
      G   A
I got a dirty down addiction, it doesn't leave a track,
      G     E
I got a Jones for your affection like a monkey on my back,
           B
There ain't no paramedic gonna save this heart attack.
              E5
When you need (that's what you get for falling in love),
              E5
Then you bleed,
                   F#5
When you're on your knees (that's what you get for falling in love),
      D                          B
Now this boy's addicted 'cause your kiss is the drug.
```

Chorus 3
```
      E               A    E
Your love is like bad medicine,
      A               E
Bad medicine is what I need,
                       A   E
Oh, shake it up, just like bad medicine,
      A                     E
So let's play doctor, baby, cure my disease.
```

```
      G    A   E
Bad, bad medicine (that's what I want),
      G    A   E
Bad, bad, medicine (oh look out me).
```

Guitar solo
```
| A     | A     | E     | E     |

| A     | A     | B     | B     |
```

```
      E
I need a respirator 'cause I'm running out of breath,

Oh you're an all-night generator wrapped in stockings and a dress.
      B
When you find your medicine you take what you can get,
                     E5  N.C.
'Cause if there's something better, baby, well they haven't found it yet.
```

Chorus 4   As Chorus 1

Chorus 5

    E   A   E
Your love is like bad medicine,

    A   E
Bad medicine is what I need,

                      A   E
Oh, shake it up, just like bad medicine,

    A   E
Your love's the potion that can cure my disease.

    G   A   E
Bad, bad medicine (that's what I want),

    G   A   E
Bad, bad medicine (who cares, who cares?)

    G   A   G5 F#5 E5   G5 F#5 E5
Bad, bad,

I've gotta do it again,

Wait a minute, wait a minute, hold on,

                                          G5 F#5 E5   G5 F#5 E5
I'm not done, one more time with feel.

Chorus 6

                    A   E
Your love is like bad medicine,

    A   E
Bad medicine is what I need,

                      A   E
Oh, shake it up, just like bad medicine,

    A   E
You've got the potion that can cure my disease.

Repeat Chorus 6 to fade

BLAZE OF GLORY

Words & Music by Jon Bon Jovi

Dm   C   G   D5   F   D

Verse 1

Dm
I wake up in the morning
   C
And I raise my weary head,
       G
I've got an old coat for a pillow
    Dm
And the earth was last night's bed.
  F
I don't know where I'm going,
   C
Only God knows where I've been,
  G
I'm a devil on the run, a six-gun lover,
  Dm   **D5**
A candle in the wind, yeah!

Verse 2

      Dm
When you're brought into this world
  C
They say you're born in sin,
   G
Well at least they gave me something
      Dm
I didn't have to steal or have to win.
     F
Well they tell me that I'm wanted,
   C
Yeah, I'm a wanted man,
  G
I'm a colt in your stable,

I'm what Cain was to Abel,
   Dm
Mister, catch me if you can.

Chorus 1

           G   **D**
I'm going down in a blaze of glory,

        G   **D**
Take me now but know the truth,

         G   **D**
I'm going out in a blaze of glory,

               C
Good Lord I never drew first but I drew first blood,

      G   **D5**
I'm going son, call me Young Gun.

Verse 3

        Dm
You ask about conscience

      C
And I offer you my soul,

          G
You ask if I'll grow to be a wise man,

        Dm
Well I ask if I'll grow old.

       F
You ask me if I've known love

            C
And what it's like to sing songs in the rain,

      G
Well I've seen love come, I've seen it shot down,

        Dm
I've seen it die in vain.

Chorus 2

      G   **D**
Shot down in a blaze of glory,

         G   **D**
Take me now but know the truth,

            G   **D**
'Cause I'm going down in a blaze of glory,

        C
Lord I never drew first but I drew first blood,

      G   **D5**
I'm the devil's son, call me Young Gun.

Guitar solo   ‖ **G** | **D** | **G** | **D** |

                 | **G** | **D** | **F** | **G**   ‖ **D5** |

Continued on next page...

Verse 4

Dm
Each night I go to bed

    C
I pray the Lord my soul to keep,

     G
No, I ain't looking for forgiveness

    Dm
But before I'm six feet deep,

    F
Lord, I got to ask a favour,

    C
And I hope you'll understand,

     G
'Cause I've lived life to the fullest,

    Dm
Let this boy die like a man,

G
Staring down a bullet,

    Dm   N.C.
Let me make my final stand.

Chorus 3

    G   D
Shot down in a blaze of glory,

    G   D
Take me now but know the truth,

     G   D
I'm going out in a blaze of glory,

    C
Lord I never drew first but I drew first blood,

     G
And I'm no-one's son.

         D   C
Call me Young Gun, oh, oh, oh,

       G   D
I'm a Young Gun, Young Gun,

    D   C
Young Gun, yeah, yeah, yeah,

    G   D5
Young Gun.

LIVIN' ON A PRAYER

Words & Music by Jon Bon Jovi, Richie Sambora & Desmond Child

Em   C/E   D/E   C   D   G

Verse 1

Em
Tommy used to work on the docks,

                                                   C/E   D/E
Union's been on strike, he's down on his luck, it's tough,

Em
So tough.

Gina works the diner all day,

                                                   C/E   D/E
Working for her man, she brings home her pay for love,

Em
For love.

Bridge 1

                  C   D   Em
She says we've got to hold on to what we've got,

     C   D   Em
It doesn't make a difference if we make it or not,

        C   D   Em   C
We've got each other and that's a lot for love,

      D
We'll give it a shot.

Chorus 1

Em C   D
Oh,   we're half way there,

G   C D
Oh,   livin' on a prayer,

Em   C   D
Take my hand, we'll make it I swear,

G   C D   Em
Oh,   livin' on a prayer.

Verse 2

Em
Tommy got his six-string in hock,

                                                     C/E   D/E
Now he's holding in when he used to make it talk so tough,

    Em
It's tough.

Gina dreams of running away,

                                                     C/E   D/E
When she cries in the night Tommy whispers "Baby, it's o.k."

      Em
Some day.

Bridge 2   As Bridge 1

Chorus 2

Em C   D
Oh, we're half way there,

G C D
Oh, livin' on a prayer,

Em   C   D
Take my hand, we'll make it I swear,

G C D
Oh, livin' on a prayer,

C
Livin' on a prayer.

Guitar solo | Em C | D | G C | D |

                | Em C | D | G C | Em |

Em   C D   Em
We've got to hold on, ready or not,

     C   D
You live for the fight when that's all you've got.

Ad lib. to fade

BROWN SUGAR

Words & Music by Mick Jagger & Keith Richards

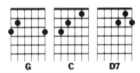

G   C   D7

G
Gold Coast slave, ship bound for cotton fields

C
Sold in a market down in New Orleans

G
Scarred old slaver know he's doin' all right

D7   **G**
Hear him whip the women just around midnight.

Chorus

D7   **G**   **C**   **G** **C**
Ah, brown sugar, how come you taste so good?

G **D7**   **G**   **C**   **G** **C G**
Ah,   brown sugar, just like a young girl should.

G
Drums beating, cold English blood runs hot

C
Lady of the house wonderin' where it's gonna stop

G
Houseboy knows that he's doin' all right

D7   **G**
You should have heard him just around midnight.

Chorus

D7   **G**
Ah, brown sugar. . .

G
I bet your Mama was a tent show queen

      C
And all her girlfriends were sweet sixteen

G
I'm no schoolboy, but I know what I like

D7   **G**
You should have heard me just around midnight.

Chorus

D7   **G**
Ah, brown sugar. . .

19TH NERVOUS BREAKDOWN

Words & Music by Mick Jagger & Keith Richards

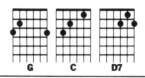

G   C   D7

G
You're the kind of person you meet

At certain dismal, dull affairs

Centre of a crowd, talking much too loud

Running up and down the stairs
C
Well it seems to me that you have seen

Too much in too few years
G
And though you've tried, you just can't hide

Your eyes are edged with tears.

Chorus
G   **D7**   **C**
You better stop, look around
           G **D7**   **G**
Here it comes, here it comes
        C
Here it comes, here it comes
        G
Here comes your nineteenth nervous breakdown.

        G
When you were a child you were treated kind

But never brought up right

You were overspoilt with a thousand toys

And still you cried all night
       C
Your mother who neglected you

Owes a million dollars tax
      G
Your father's still perfecting ways

Of making sealing wax.

Chorus
G   **D7**
You better stop. . . .

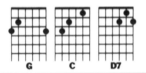

G   C   D7

D7   **G**
Oh who's to blame, that girl's just insane

Well nothing I do don't seem to work
    D7
It only seems to make matters worse

Oh please.

       G
You were still in school when you had that fool

Who really messed your mind

And after that, you turned your back

On treating people kind
    C
On our first trip I tried so hard

To rearrange your mind
    G
But after a while I realised

You were disarranging mine.

Chorus
        D7
You better stop. . . .

D7   **G**
Oh who's to blame, that girl's just insane

Well nothing I do don't seem to work
    D7
It only seems to make matters worse

Oh please.

ALL AROUND THE WORLD

Words & Music by Noel Gallagher

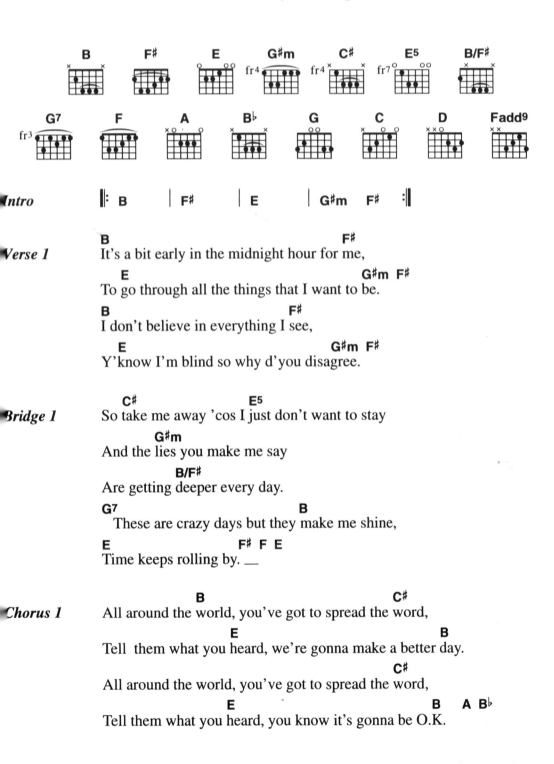

Intro

|: B | F♯ | E | G♯m F♯ :|

Verse 1

B   F♯
It's a bit early in the midnight hour for me,

  E   G♯m F♯
To go through all the things that I want to be.

B   F♯
I don't believe in everything I see,

  E   G♯m F♯
Y'know I'm blind so why d'you disagree.

Bridge 1

    C♯   E5
So take me away 'cos I just don't want to stay

    G♯m
And the lies you make me say

    B/F♯
Are getting deeper every day.

G7   B
 These are crazy days but they make me shine,

E   F♯ F E
Time keeps rolling by. —

Chorus 1

         B   C♯
All around the world, you've got to spread the word,

        E   B
Tell them what you heard, we're gonna make a better day.

              C♯
All around the world, you've got to spread the word,

       E   B A B♭
Tell them what you heard, you know it's gonna be O.K.

Verse 2
```
          B                                        F#
So what you gonna do when the walls come falling down?
            E                          G#m F#
You never move, you never make a sound.
          B                                 F#
Where you gonna swim with the riches that you found?
               E                       G#m     F#
If you're lost at sea I hope that you've drowned.
```

Bridge 2   As Bridge 1

Chorus 2
```
                   B                          C#
All around the world, you've got to spread the word,
                    E                             B
Tell  them what you heard, we're gonna make a better day.
                                        C#
All around the world, you've got to spread the word,
                    E                           B
Tell them what you heard, you know it's gonna be O.K.
```

Chorus 3
```
         B           C#
Na na na, na na na na,
            E        B
Na na na na, na na na.
                    C#
Na na na, na na na na,
            E        B        E
Na na na na, na na na, ___ ah.
B      E     B     E
Na  -  ah,    na  -  ah.
G                         E
Na na na na, na na na na.
G                         E
Na na na na, na na na na.
G                         E
Na na na na, na na na na.
G
Na na na na, na na na na, na na na na na.
```

Chorus 4
```
                   C                          D
All around the world, you've gotta spread the word,
                 Fadd9                           C
Tell 'em what you heard, you're gonna make a better day.
                                              D
'Cos all around the world, you've gotta spread the word,
                 Fadd9                          C
Tell 'em what you heard, you know it's gonna be O.K.
```

Chorus 5

         C   **D**
All around the world, you've gotta spread the word,

                Fadd⁹   **C**
Tell 'em what you heard, you're gonna make a better day.

                                   D
'Cos all around the world, you've gotta spread the word,

                Fadd⁹   **C**
Tell 'em what you heard, you know it's gonna be O.K.

‖: **A**   **G**   **A**
            It's gonna be O.K. :‖

A   **G**   **A**
          It's gonna be O.K.   It's gonna be O.K.

Chorus 6

                   D   **E**
‖: All around the world, you've gotta spread the word,

                  G   **D**
Tell 'em what you heard, you're gonna make a better day.

                               E
'Cos all around the world, you've gotta spread the word,

                  G   **D**
Tell 'em what you heard, you know it's gonna be O.K. :‖

Outro

D   **E**   **G**   **D**
La la la,   la la la,   la la, — la la la la,   la. —

D   **E**   **G**   **D**
La la la,   la la la,   la la, — la la la la,   la. —

       D   **E**
And I know what I know, what I know, what I know,

         G   **D**
Yeah, I know what I know, it's gonna be O.K.

       D   **E**
And I know what I know, what I know, what I know,

         G   **D**
Yeah, I know what I know, it's gonna be O.K.

       D   **E**
Yeah I know what I know, and I know what I know,

         G   **D**
Yeah, I know what I know, it's gonna be O.K.

       D   **E**
Yeah I know what I know, and I know what I know,

         G   **D**
Yeah, I know what I know, please don't cry, never say die.

‖: **D**   **E**   **G**   **D**
  La la la,   la la la,   la la, — la la la la,   la. — :‖

                                  Repeat ad lib. to fade

BE HERE NOW

Words & Music by Noel Gallagher

B5   C#5   A5   E5   G5   Bb5

fr7   fr9   fr5   fr3   fr6

Intro

‖: B5 | B5 | B5 | C#5 A5 :‖

Verse 1

B5
Wash your face in the morning sun,
C#5   A5
Flash your pan at the song that I'm singing.
B5
Touch down bass living on the run,
C#5   A5
Make no sweat of the hole that you're digging.

| B5 | B5 | B5 | C#5 A5 ‖

Verse 2

B5
Wrap up cold when it's warm outside,
C#5   A5
Your shit jokes remind me of Digsy's.
B5
Be my magic carpet ride,
C#5 A5   B5
Fly me down to capitol city in the sun.

| B5 | B5 | C#5 A5 ‖

Chorus 1

E5   G5 A5
Kickin' up a storm
    E5   G5 A5
From the day that I was born.
E5
Sing a song for me,
G5   A5
One___ from "Let It Be"
G5
Open up yer eyes,
   A5   Bb5 | B5 | B5 | B5 | C#5 A5
Get a grip of yourself inside.

Verse 3

B5
Wash your face in the morning sun,

                  C#5   A5
Flash your pan at the song that I'm singing.

B5
Touch down bass living on the run,

                  C#5   A5
Make no sweat of the hole that you're digging.

| B5 | B5 | B5 | C#5 A5 ‖

Chorus 2

E5   G5 A5
Kickin' up a storm

         E5   G5 A5
From the day that I was born.

E5
Sing a song for me,

G5   A5
One ___ from "Let It Be"

G5
Open up yer eyes,

      A5   Bb5
Get a grip of yourself inside.

Solo

| B5 | B5 | A5 | E5 |
         Inside.   *Get a grip inside.___*

| B5 | B5 | A5 | E5 |
            Get a grip inside. ___   *You betcha!*

| B5 | B5 | A5 | E5 |

| B5 | B5 | A5 | E5 ‖

| B5 | B5 | B5 | B5 ‖

Verse 4

     B5
So wrap up cold when it's warm outside,

                  C#5   A5
Please sit down, you make me feel giddy.

B5
Be my magic carpet ride,

             C#5   A5
Fly me down to capitol city.

Chorus 3

E5   G5 A5
Kickin' up a storm

        E5   G5 A5
From the day that I was born.

E5
Sing a song for me,

G5   A5
One __ from 'Let It Be'

G5
Open up yer eyes,

       A5   B♭5
Get a grip of yourself inside.

Outro

| B5 | B5 | A5 | E5 | |

                        Get a grip inside. __

‖: B5 | B5 | A5 | E5 :‖
        Get a grip inside. __   *Get a grip inside.*

‖: B5 | B5 | A5 | E5 :‖
  C'mon, c'mon etc.   *Yeah, yeah, yeah.*

‖: B5 | B5 | A5 | E5 :‖
      Yeah, yeah, yeah.   *Yeah, yeah, yeah.*

| B5 | B5 | A5 | E5 |
  C'mon, c'mon etc.   *Yeah, yeah, yeah.*

| B5 ‖

WONDERWALL

Words & Music by Noel Gallagher

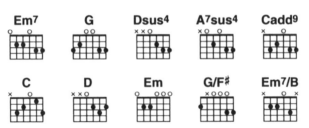

Use Capo at 2nd fret to play along with the recording

Intro ‖: Em⁷ G | Dsus⁴ | A⁷sus⁴ | Em⁷ G | Dsus⁴ | A⁷sus⁴ :‖

Verse 1

Em⁷   G
Today is gonna be the day
          Dsus⁴   A⁷sus⁴
That they're gonna throw it back to you,
Em⁷   G
By now you should have somehow
    Dsus⁴   A⁷sus⁴
Realised what you gotta do.
Em⁷   G   Dsus⁴   A⁷sus⁴
I don't believe that anybody feels the way that I do
        Cadd⁹ Dsus⁴ | A⁷sus⁴ ‖
About you now.

Verse 2

Em⁷   G
Back beat, the word is on the street
     Dsus⁴   A⁷sus⁴
That the fire in your heart is out,
Em⁷   G
I'm sure you've heard it all before,
    Dsus⁴   A⁷sus⁴
But you never really had a doubt.
Em⁷   G   Dsus⁴   A⁷sus⁴
I don't believe that anybody feels the way that I do
     Em⁷ G | Dsus⁴ A⁷sus⁴ ‖
About you now.

Bridge 1

       C   D   Em
And all the roads we have are winding,

       C   D   Em
And all the lights that lead us there are blinding,

C   D   G   G/F# Em
There are many things that I would like to say to you

           A7sus4
But I don't know how.

Chorus 1

        Cadd9   Em7 | G
Because maybe,

      Em7   Cadd9   Em7 G
You're gonna be the one that saves me,

   Em7 Cadd9 Em7 | G
And after all,

         Em7   Cadd9 Em7 | G Em7/B | N.C. A7sus4 ||
You're my wonderwall.

Verse 3

Em7   G
Today was gonna be the day,

     Dsus4   A7sus4
But they'll never throw it back at you,

Em7   G
By now you should have somehow

   Dsus4   A7sus4
Realised what you're not to do.

Em7   G   Dsus4   A7sus4
I don't believe that anybody feels the way I do

      Em7 G | Dsus4 A7sus4 ||
About you now.

Bridge 2

       C   D   Em
And all the roads that lead you there were winding,

       C   D   Em
And all the lights that light the way are blinding,

C   D   G   G/F# Em
There are many things that I would like to say to you

           A7sus4
But I don't know how.

Continued on next page...

74

Chorus 2

    Cadd⁹ **Em⁷** | **G**
I said maybe

    Em⁷   **Cadd⁹** **Em⁷** | **G**
You're gonna be the one that saves me

     Em⁷ Cadd⁹ Em⁷ | **G**
And after all

        Em⁷   **Cadd⁹ Em⁷** | **G Em⁷** ‖
You're my wonderwall.

Chorus 3   As Chorus 2

Outro

    Cadd⁹ **Em⁷** | **G**
I said maybe

    Em⁷   **Cadd⁹** **Em⁷** | **G**
You're gonna be the one that saves me,

    Em⁷   **Cadd⁹** **Em⁷** | **G**
You're gonna be the one that saves me,

    Em⁷   **Cadd⁹** **Em⁷** | **G Em⁷** ‖
You're gonna be the one that saves me.

Instrumental ‖: **Cadd⁹ Em⁷** | **G Em⁷** | **Cadd⁹ Em⁷** | **G Em⁷** :‖

MORNING GLORY

Words & Music by Noel Gallagher

| Em | Dsus2 | D5 | A7sus4 | Cadd9 | B | Asus4 |

Play 4 times

Intro

‖: Em | Em | Em | Em :‖

‖: Em | Dsus2 | Em | Dsus2 :‖

Verse 1

Em   Dsus2
All your dreams are made

        Em   Dsus2
When you're chained to the mirror on your razor blade,

   Em   Dsus2   A7sus4 Cadd9
Today's the day that all the world will see.

     Em   Dsus2
Another sunny afternoon,

Em   Dsus2
Walking to the sound of my favourite tune,

    Em   Dsus2   A7sus4 Cadd9
Tomorrow never knows what it doesn't know too soon.

Bridge 1

Dsus2   Cadd9
Need a little time to wake up,

Dsus2   Cadd9
Need a little time to wake up, wake up,

Dsus2   Cadd9
Need a little time to wake up,

D5
Need a little time to rest your mind,

   B   Em Dsus2
You know you should, so I guess you might as well.

Chorus 1

Asus⁴   **Cadd⁹**
What's the story, Morning Glory?

Em   **Dsus²**   **Asus⁴**   **Cadd⁹**
Well,   you need a little time to wake up, wake up,

Em   **Dsus²**   **Asus⁴**   **Cadd⁹**
Well,   what's the story, Morning Glory?

Em   **Dsus²**   **Asus⁴**   **Cadd⁹**
Well,   you need a little time to wake up, wake up.

Play 4 times

Instrumental ‖: **Em** | **Em** | **Em** | **Em**   :‖

‖: **Em** | **Dsus²** | **Em** | **Dsus²**   :‖

Verse 3   As Verse 1

Bridge 2   As Bridge 1

Chorus 2   As Chorus 1

Chorus 3   As Chorus 1

Outro   ‖: **Em** | **Dsus²** | **Em** | **Dsus²**   :‖   *Repeat to fade*

CAN'T STAND LOSING YOU

Words & Music by Sting

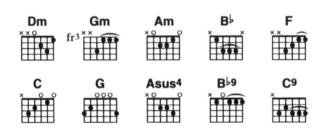

Intro

| Dm Gm | Dm Gm | Dm Gm | Dm Gm ||

Verse 1

Dm   Am Gm
Called you so many times today

   Dm   Am   Gm
And I guess it's all true what your girl friends say,

   Dm Am   Gm
That you don't ever want so see me again,

    Dm   Am   Gm
And your brother's gonna kill me and he's six foot ten,

  Bb   F Bb   F
I guess you'd call it cowardice

     C   G   C   Asus4
But I'm not prepared to go on like this.

Chorus 1

  Bb
I can't, I can't, I can't stand losing,

 Gm
I can't, I can't, I can't stand losing,

Asus4   Dm Gm
I can't, I can't, I can't, I can't stand losing you,

Dm   Gm Dm   Gm
  I can't stand losing you,

Dm Gm   Dm   Gm
  I can't stand losing you,

Dm Gm   Dm   Gm   Dm Gm
  I can't stand losing you.

Verse 2

    Dm   **Am**   **Gm**
I see you've sent my letters back,

         Dm Am   **Gm**
And my L.P. records and they're all scratched.

    Dm   **Am**   **Gm**
I can't see the point in another day,

       Dm   **Am**   **Gm**
When nobody listens to a word I say.

        B♭   **F**   **B♭**   **F**
You can call it lack of confidence

       C   **G**   **C**   **Asus4**
But to carry on living doesn't make no sense.

Chorus 2

    B♭
I can't, I can't, I can't stand losing,

    Gm
I can't, I can't, I can't stand losing,

    Asus4
I can't, I can't, I can't stand losing,

    B♭
I can't, I can't, I can't stand losing,

    Gm
I can't, I can't, I can't stand losing,

    Asus4
I can't, I can't, I can't stand losing.

Instrumental ‖: **B♭9** | **B♭9** | **C9** | **C9** :‖

Middle

    Dm
I guess this is our last goodbye,

And you don't care so I won't cry,

And you'll be sorry when I'm dead

And all this guilt will blow your head.

    B♭   **F**   **B♭** **F**
I guess you'd call it suicide

      C   **G**   **C**   **Asus4**
But I'm too full to swallow my pride.

Chorus 3

    B♭
I can't, I can't, I can't stand losing,

    Gm
I can't, I can't, I can't stand losing,

    Asus⁴
I can't, I can't, I can't stand losing,

    B♭
I can't, I can't, I can't stand losing,

    Gm
I can't, I can't, I can't stand losing,

    Asus⁴
I can't, I can't, I can't stand losing,

Outro

     C
‖: I can't, I can't, I can't stand losing,

    Asus⁴
I can't, I can't, I can't stand losing,

    B♭
I can't, I can't, I can't stand losing. :‖ *Repeat to fade*

EVERY BREATH YOU TAKE

Words & Music by Sting

Gadd9   Emadd9   Csus2   Dsus2   Csus2/B♭   Aadd9   E♭   F

Intro | Gadd9 | Gadd9 | Emadd9 | Emadd9 |

| Csus2 | Dsus2 | Gadd9 |

Verse 1

Gadd9
    Ev'ry breath you take,
      Emadd9
Ev'ry move you make,
        Csus2
Ev'ry bone you break,
      Dsus2
Ev'ry step you take,
        Emadd9
I'll be watching you.

      Gadd9
Ev'ry single day,
      Emadd9
Ev'ry word you say,
      Csus2
Ev'ry game you play,
      Dsus2
Ev'ry night you stay,
      Gadd9
I'll be watching you.

Chorus 1

            Csus²
Oh, can't you see

Csus²/B♭   **Gadd⁹**
You belong to me,

                Aadd⁹
How my poor heart aches

             Dsus²
With ev'ry step you take.

          Gadd⁹
Ev'ry move you make,

          Emadd⁹
Ev'ry vow you break,

             Csus²
Ev'ry smile you fake,

             Dsus²
Ev'ry claim you stake

                Emadd⁹
I'll be watching you.

Middle

E♭
  Since you've gone, I've been lost without a trace,

F
  I dream at night I can only see your face,

E♭
  I look around but it's you I can't replace,

F
  I feel so cold and I long for your embrace,

E♭
  I keep crying baby, baby please.

Instrumental ‖: **Gadd⁹** | **Gadd⁹** | **Emadd⁹** | **Emadd⁹** |

           | **Csus²** | **Dsus²** | **Gadd⁹** | **Gadd⁹** :‖

Chorus 2   As Chorus 1

Outro

Emadd⁹   **Csus²**
Ev'ry move you make,

             Dsus²
Ev'ry step you take

                Emadd⁹
I'll be watching you.

Emadd⁹
          I'll be watching

‖: **Gadd⁹**   **Gadd⁹**   **Emadd⁹** **Csus²**
   you. | | | I'll be watching :‖ *Repeat to fade*

SEVEN DAYS

Words & Music by Sting

C6/9   Eb6/9#11   Bb6/9   G   F

E   F#m7b5   E7/G#   Am7   Bb7#11   Fm(maj7)

Intro

‖: C6/9 | C6/9 | C6/9 | C6/9 :‖

Verse 1

C6/9
Seven days was all she wrote,
Eb6/9#11   Bb6/9
　A kind of ultimatum note,
　　　G   F
She gave to me, she gave to me.
C6/9
When I thought the field had cleared,
　Eb6/9#11   Bb6/9
It seems another suit appeared
　　　G   E
To challenge me, woe is me.

Verse 2

C6/9
Though I hate to make a choice,
　　Eb6/9#11   Bb6/9
My options are decreasing
　　　G   F
Mostly rapidly, well, we'll see.
C6/9
I don't think she'd bluff this time,
　Eb6/9#11   Bb6/9
I really have to make her mine,
　　　G   E
It's plain to see, it's him or me.

Chorus 1

    F   F#m7♭5   G
Monday, I could wait till Tuesday

       E7/G#   Am7
If I make up my mind,

    F   G
Wednesday would be fine,

    E7/G#   Am7
Thursday's on my mind,

    B♭7#11   Am7
Friday'd give me time,

    B♭7#11   Am7
Saturday could wait

       Fm(maj7)   C6/9
But Sunday'd be to late.

Verse 3

C6/9
The fact he's over six feet ten

         E♭6/9#11   B♭6/9
Might instill fear in other men

    G   F
But not in me, the mighty flea.

C6/9
Ask if I am mouse or man,

       E♭6/9#11   B♭6/9
The mirror squeaked, away I ran.

       G   E
He'll murder me, in time for his tea.

Verse 4

C6/9
Does it bother me at all,

      E♭6/9#11 B♭6/9
My rival is neanderthal,

    G   F
It makes me think, perhaps I need a drink.

C6/9
I.Q. is no problem here,

      E♭6/9#11   B♭6/9
We won't be playing Scrabble

      G   E
For her hand I fear, I need that beer.

Chorus 2   As Chorus 1

Bridge

B♭6/9#11   C6/9
  Seven days will quickly go,
B♭6/9#11   C6/9
  The fact remains I love her so.
B♭6/9#11   F
  Seven days, so many ways,
B♭6/9#11   C6/9
  But I can't run away,
B♭6/9#11   C6/9
  I can't run away.

Chorus 3

F   F#m7♭5   G
Monday, I could wait till Tuesday
 E7/G#   Am7
If I make up my mind.
F   G
Wednesday would be fine,
E7/G#   Am7
Thursday's on my mind.
B♭7#11   Am7
Friday'd give me time,
B♭7#11   Am7
Saturday could wait,
B♭9#11 | C6/9 | C6/9 | B♭7#11 | B♭7#11 |
Sunday'd be too late,
| C6/9 | C6/9 | B♭7#11
      Sunday'd be too late.

Outro

   C6/9
Do I have to tell a story
  B♭7#11
Of a thousand rainy days since we first met.

| C6/9 | C6/9 | B♭7#11 | B♭7#11 |
   C6/9
It's a big enough umbrella
   B♭7#11
But it's always me that ends up getting
| C6/9 | C6/9 | B♭7#11 | B♭7#11 | C6/9 ‖
Wet,   yeah,   yeah, ⎯⎯⎯   oh!

5TH SEASON

Words & Music by Paul Weller

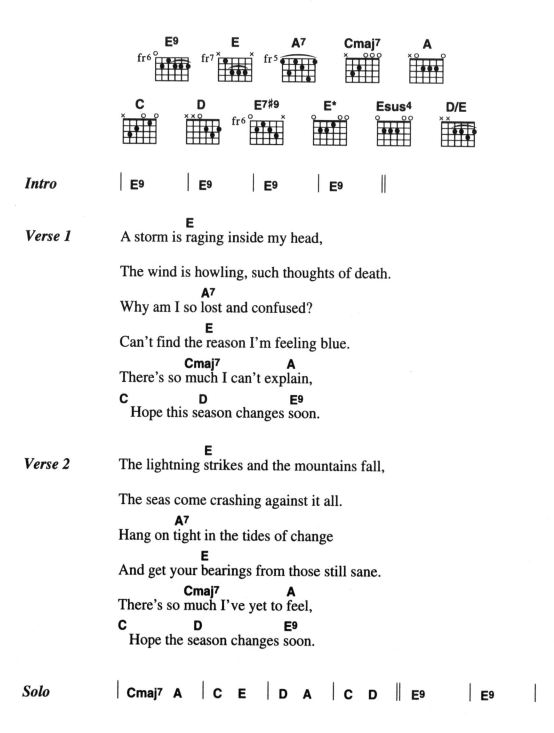

Intro | E9 | E9 | E9 | E9 ‖

Verse 1

         E
A storm is raging inside my head,

The wind is howling, such thoughts of death.
       A7
Why am I so lost and confused?
         E
Can't find the reason I'm feeling blue.
      Cmaj7   **A**
There's so much I can't explain,
C   **D**   **E9**
  Hope this season changes soon.

Verse 2

         E
The lightning strikes and the mountains fall,

The seas come crashing against it all.
       A7
Hang on tight in the tides of change
         E
And get your bearings from those still sane.
      Cmaj7   **A**
There's so much I've yet to feel,
C   **D**   **E9**
  Hope the season changes soon.

Solo | Cmaj7 A | C E | D A | C D ‖ E9 | E9 |

Verse 3

           E7#9
The serpent tangles in the lion's claw,

A cloud of darkness hangs over all.
     A7
As fires burn in search of sky,
     E7#9
So blow embers like fire flies.
       Cmaj7   **A**
I'm hoping love is where they'll lie,
C   **D**   **E9**
  And the season change us too.

Solo

| E9 | E9 | E9 | E9 |

| A7 | A7 | E9 | E9 |

| Cmaj7 A | C D | E7#9 | E7#9 ||

Verse 4

          E7#9
The lightning strikes, oh, and the mountains fall,

The seas come crashing against it all.
     A7
Hang on tight in the tides of change
       E7#9
And get your bearings from those still sane.
      Cmaj7   **A**
I'm hoping love is where they say,
C   **D**   **E7#9**
  Hope the season changes too.
      Cmaj7   **A**
I'm hoping love is where they'll lie,
C   **D**   **E7#9**
  And the season change us too.

Solo

| Cmaj7 A | C E | D A | C D | E7#9 | E7#9 ||

||: E9 | E9 | E9 | E9 |

| A7 | A7 | E9 | E9 |

| Cmaj7 A | C D | E9 | E9 :||

| Esus4 E* | E* | Esus4 E* | E* | Esus4 E* | D/E ||

89

HAS MY FIRE REALLY GONE OUT?

Words & Music by Paul Weller

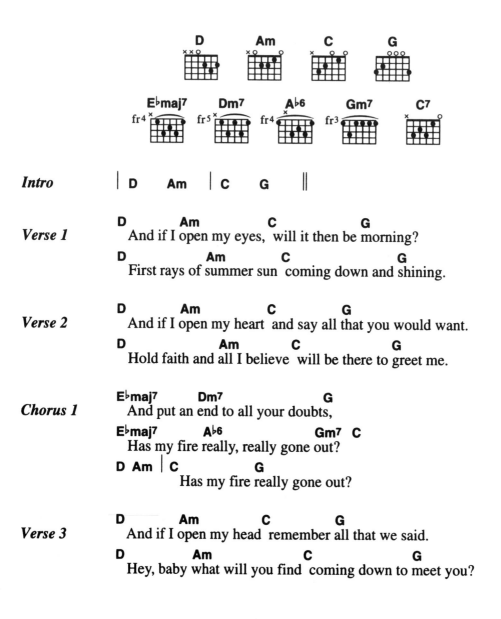

Intro | D Am | C G ‖

Verse 1
D   Am   C   G
And if I open my eyes, will it then be morning?
D   Am   C   G
First rays of summer sun coming down and shining.

Verse 2
D   Am   C   G
And if I open my heart and say all that you would want.
D   Am   C   G
Hold faith and all I believe will be there to greet me.

Chorus 1
E♭maj7   Dm7   G
And put an end to all your doubts,
E♭maj7   A♭6   Gm7 C
Has my fire really, really gone out?
D Am | C   G
        Has my fire really gone out?

Verse 3
D   Am   C   G
And if I open my head remember all that we said.
D   Am   C   G
Hey, baby what will you find coming down to meet you?

Middle 1

C7   G
A lot of words but no-one talking,

C7   G
I don't want no part of that.

C7   G
Something real is what I'm seeking,

C7   G
One clear voice in the wilderness.

D Am | C   G   D Am | C G
          Has my fire really gone out?

Chorus 2

E♭maj7   Dm7   G
And put an end to all your doubts,

E♭maj7   A♭6   Gm7 G C
Has my fire really, really gone out?

E♭maj7   Dm7   G
And put an end to all your doubts,

E♭maj7   A♭6   Gm7 C
Has my fire really, really gone out?

Verse 4   As Verse 1

Verse 5   As Verse 2

Middle 2 | C7 G | C7 G |

C7   G
Something real is what I'm seeking,

C7   G
One clear voice in the wilderness.

Ad lib. to end

Instrumental | C7 G | C7 G | C7 G | C7 G | G | G ||

DON'T LET ME DOWN

Words & Music by John Lennon & Paul McCartney

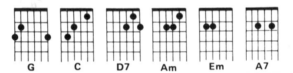

G   C   D7   Am   Em   A7

G   **Am**
Nobody ever loved me like she does
             G
Oo she does, yes she does
                  Am
And if somebody loved me like she do me
           G
Oo she do me, yes she does.

Chorus
       Am   **G**
Don't let me down, don't let me down
       Am   **G**
Don't let me down, don't let me down.

G
I'm in love for the first time
            D7
Don't you know it's gonna last

It's a love that lasts forever
           G
It's a love that had no past.

Chorus
       Am
Don't let me down. . . .

G   **Am**
And from the first time that she really done me

           G
Oo she done me, she done me good
          Am
I guess nobody ever really done me
          G
Oo she done me, she done me good.

Chorus
       Am
Don't let me down. . . .

GOLDEN SLUMBERS

Words & Music by John Lennon & Paul McCartney

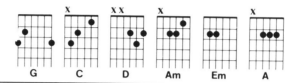

G   C   D   Am   Em   A

Em
Once there was a way
       Am
To get back homeward.
D
Once there was a way
       G
To get back home

D   **Em**   **Am**
Sleep pretty darling do not cry,
D   **G**
And I will sing a lullaby.
     C   **G**
Golden slumbers fill your eyes,
     C   **G**
Smiles awake you when you rise.
D   **Em**   **Am**
Sleep pretty darling do not cry,
D   **G**
And I will sing a lullaby.

Em
Once there was a way
       Am
To get back homeward.
D
Once there was a way
       G
To get back home
D   **Em**   **Am**
Sleep pretty darling do not cry,
D   **G**
And I will sing a lullaby.

LOVE ME DO

Words & Music by John Lennon & Paul McCartney

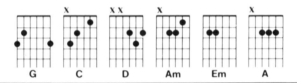

G   C   D   Am   Em   A

G   **C**   **G**   **C**
Love, love me do, you know I love you.
   G   **C**
I'll always be true, so please –
       G
Love me do.
C **G**
Oo – Love me do.

G   **C**   **G**   **C**
Love, love me do, you know I love you,
   G   **C**
I'll always be true, so please –
       G
Love me do.
C **G**
Oo – Love me do.

D   **C**   **G**
Someone to love, somebody new.
D   **C** **G**
Someone to love, someone like you.

G   **C**   **G**   **C**
Love, love me do, you know I love you.
   G   **C**
I'll always be true, so please –
       G
Love me do.

Repeat 'till fade
C   **G**
Ooh love me do . . .

GOOD MORNING, GOOD MORNING

Words & Music by John Lennon & Paul McCartney

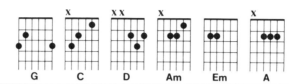

G   C   D   Am   Em   A

    A   **D**   **A**
Good morning, good morning, good morning,
    D   **A**
Good morning, good morning – a.

A   **G**
Nothing to do to save his life, call his wife in.
A   **G**   **A**
Nothing to say but "What a day, how's your boy been?"
D   **Em**
Nothing to do it's up to you.
    A   **G**
I've got nothing to say but it's O.K.
    A   **D**   **A**
Good morning, good morning, good morning – a.

A   **G**
Going to work don't want to go,

Feeling low down.
A   **G**
Heading for home you start to roam,
        A   **D**
Then you're in town.

A   **D**   **A**
Ev'rybody knows there's nothing doing,
        D   **A**
Ev'rything is closed it's like a ruin,
        D   **A**
Ev'ryone you see is half asleep,
              D   **A**
And you're on your own, you're in the street.

A   **G**
After a while you start to smile, now you feel cool.
A   **G**   **A**
Then you decide to take a walk by the old school.
D   **E**
Nothing has changed it's still the same
    A   **G**
I've got nothing to say but it's O.K.
    A   **D**   **A**
Good morning, good morning, good morning – a.

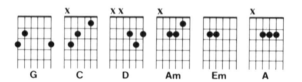

G   C   D   Am   Em   A

A   **D**   **A**
People running round it's five o'clock.
            D   **A**
Ev'rywhere in town it's getting dark.
             D   **A**
Ev'ryone you see is full of life.
             D   **A**
It's time for tea and meet the wife.

     A   **G**
Somebody needs to know the time, glad that I'm here.
A   **G**   **A**
Watching the skirts, you start to flirt, now you're in gear.
D   **E**
Go to a show you hope she goes.
     A   **G**
I've got nothing to say but it's O.K.
     A   **D**   **A**
Good morning, good morning, good morning – a.

Repeat 'till fade

               D   **A**
Good morning, good morning, good morning – a.

THE BEST GUITAR CHORD
SONGBOOK EVER!

CONTENTS

ALL I REALLY WANT

Music by Alanis Morissette and Glenn Ballard ▪ Lyrics by Alanis Morissette

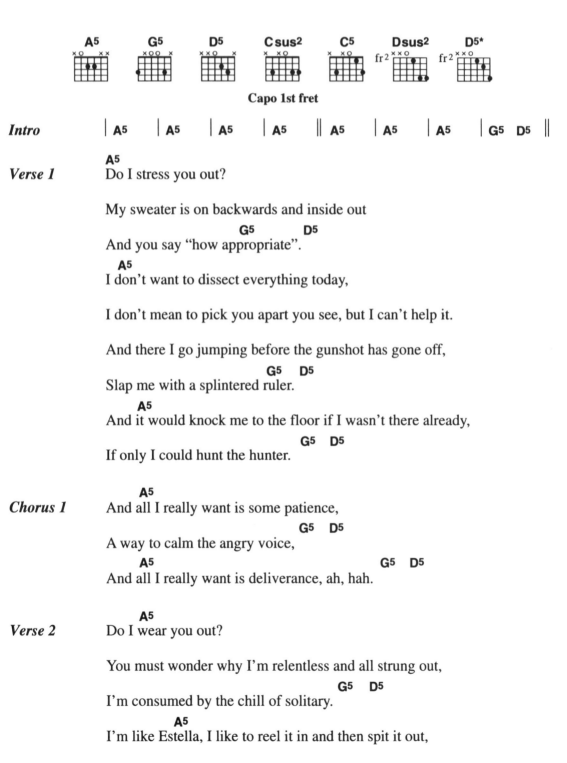

Capo 1st fret

Intro | A5 | A5 | A5 | A5   ‖ A5 | A5 | A5 | G5 D5 ‖

Verse 1
A5
Do I stress you out?

My sweater is on backwards and inside out
          G5   **D5**
And you say "how appropriate".
    A5
I don't want to dissect everything today,

I don't mean to pick you apart you see, but I can't help it.

And there I go jumping before the gunshot has gone off,
          G5   **D5**
Slap me with a splintered ruler.
      A5
And it would knock me to the floor if I wasn't there already,
          G5   **D5**
If only I could hunt the hunter.

Chorus 1
      A5
And all I really want is some patience,
          G5   **D5**
A way to calm the angry voice,
      A5   **G5**   **D5**
And all I really want is deliverance, ah, hah.

Verse 2
      A5
Do I wear you out?

You must wonder why I'm relentless and all strung out,
          G5   **D5**
I'm consumed by the chill of solitary.
          A5
I'm like Estella, I like to reel it in and then spit it out,

101

(cont)

                                            G5 D5

I'm frustrated by your apathy.

        A5

And I am frightened by the corrupted ways of this land,

                          G5 D5

If only I could meet the maker.

        A5

And I am fascinated by the spiritual man,

                               G5 D5

I am humbled by his humble nature,   yeah.

Chorus 2

        A5

And what I wouldn't give to find a soulmate,

                            G5 D5

Someone else to catch this drift,

        A5   **G5 D5**

And what I wouldn't give to meet a kindred, ah, hah.

Interlude | **A5** | **A5** | **A5** | **G5 D5** ‖

Middle

   Csus2   **C5**   **Dsus2**   **D5***

Enough about me, let's talk about you for a minute.

   Csus2   **C5**   **Dsus2** **D5***

Enough about you, let's talk about life for a while.

     Csus2 **C5**   **Dsus2**   **D5***

The conflicts, the craziness and the sound of pretences falling

    A5

All around, all around.

Verse 3

   (A5)

Why are you so petrified of silence?

                       N.C.

Here, can you handle this?

                A5

Did you think about bills, your ex, your deadlines,

Or when you think you're gonna die?

Or did you long for the next distraction?

And all I need now is intellectual intercourse,

                        G5   **D5**

A soul to dig the hole much deeper.

     A5

And I have no concept of time other than it is flying,

                    G5 D5

If only I could kill the killer.

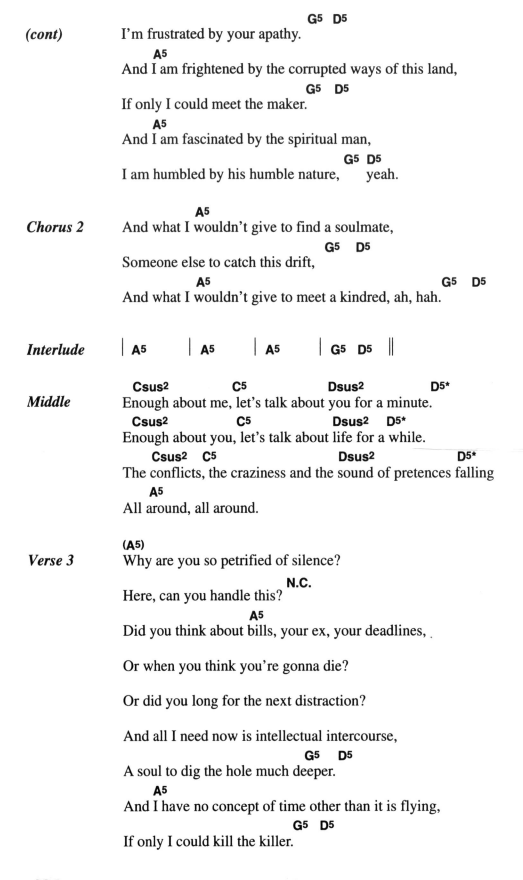

Chorus 3   𝄆 And all I really want is some peace, man,

                            G5 D5

A place to find a common ground,

         A5   **G5 D5**

And all I really want is a wavelength, ah, hah.

         A5

And all I really want is some comfort,

                         G5 D5

A way to get my hands untied,

         A5   **G5 D5**

And all I really want is some justice, ah, hah. 𝄇

Repeat to fade
with ad lib. vocals

HAND IN MY POCKET

Music by Alanis Morissette and Glenn Ballard ▪ Lyrics by Alanis Morissette

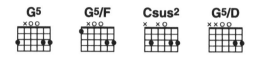

Intro | G5 | G5 | G5 | G5 ‖

Verse 1

G5
I'm broke but I'm happy, I'm poor but I'm kind,

I'm short but I'm healthy, yeah.

I'm high but I'm grounded, I'm sane but I'm overwhelmed,

I'm lost but I'm hopeful baby.

Chorus 1

                             G5/F   **Csus2**
And what it all comes down to

                         G5
Is that everything's gonna be fine, fine, fine,

         G5/F
'Cause I got one hand in my pocket

       Csus2   **G5/D**   **G5**
And the other one is giving a high five.

Verse 2

G5
I feel drunk but I'm sober, I'm young and I'm underpaid,

I'm tired but I'm working, yeah.

I care but I'm restless, I'm here but I'm really gone,

I'm wrong and I'm sorry baby.

Chorus 2   **G5/F**   **Csus2**
And what it all comes down to

                                    G5
Is that everything's gonna be quite alright,

                   G5/F
'Cos I've got one hand in my pocket

              Csus2   **G5/D**   **G5**
And the other one is flicking a cigarette.

Solo | **G5** | **G5** | **G5** | **G5** | **G5** | **G5** | **G5** | **G5** ||

Chorus 3   **G5/F**   **Csus2**
And what it all comes down to

                           G5
Is that I haven't got it all figured out just yet,

                   G5/F
'Cos I've got one hand in my pocket

              Csus2   **G5/D**   **G5**
And the other one is giving a peace sign.

          G5
Verse 3   I'm free but I'm focused, I'm green but I'm wise,

               I'm hard but I'm friendly baby.

               I'm sad but I'm laughing, I'm brave but I'm chicken shit,

               I'm sick but I'm pretty baby.

Chorus 4   **G5/F**   **Csus2**
And what it all boils down to

                           G5
Is that no one's got it figured out just yet.

                   G5/F
But I've got one hand in my pocket

              Csus2   **G5/D**   **G5**
And the other one is playing a piano.

                         G5/F   **Csus2**
And what it all comes down to my friends

                       G5
Is that every thing is just fine, fine, fine,

                   G5/F
'Cos I've got one hand in my pocket

              Csus2   **G5/D**   **G5**
And the other one is hailing a taxi cab.

IRONIC

Music by Alanis Morissette and Glenn Ballard ▪ Lyrics by Alanis Morissette

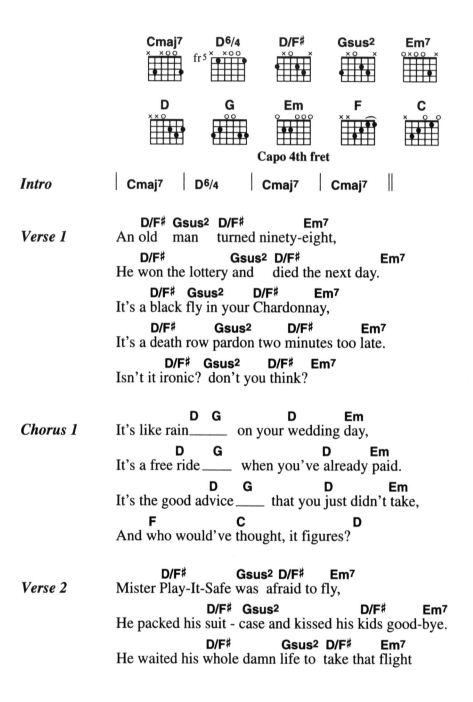

Capo 4th fret

Intro | Cmaj7 | D6/4 | Cmaj7 | Cmaj7 ‖

Verse 1

D/F♯ Gsus2 D/F♯   Em7
An old man   turned ninety-eight,

D/F♯   Gsus2 D/F♯   Em7
He won the lottery and   died the next day.

D/F♯ Gsus2   D/F♯   Em7
It's a black fly in your Chardonnay,

D/F♯   Gsus2   D/F♯   Em7
It's a death row pardon two minutes too late.

D/F♯ Gsus2   D/F♯ Em7
Isn't it ironic? don't you think?

Chorus 1

D   G   D   Em
It's like rain_____ on your wedding day,

D   G   D   Em
It's a free ride____ when you've already paid.

D   G   D   Em
It's the good advice____ that you just didn't take,

F   C   D
And who would've thought, it figures?

Verse 2

D/F♯   Gsus2 D/F♯   Em7
Mister Play-It-Safe was afraid to fly,

D/F♯ Gsus2   D/F♯   Em7
He packed his suit - case and kissed his kids good-bye.

D/F♯   Gsus2 D/F♯   Em7
He waited his whole damn life to take that flight

cont.

      D/F#   **Gsus²**
And as the plane crashed down he thought,
     D/F#   **Em⁷**
"Well isn't this nice?"
        D/F# **Gsus²**   **D/F#** **Em⁷**
And isn't it ironic? don't you think?

Chorus 2   As Chorus 1

        Cmaj⁷

Bridge   Well life has a funny way of sneaking up
D⁶ᐟ⁴
On you when you think everything's okay and
Cmaj⁷   **D⁶ᐟ⁴**
Everything's going right.
        Cmaj⁷
And life has a funny way of helping you
D⁶ᐟ⁴
Out when you think everything's going wrong and
Cmaj⁷
Everything blows up in your face.

        D/F# **Gsus²**   **D/F#**   **Em⁷**

Verse 3   A traffic jam when you're already late,
        D/F#   **Gsus²**   **D/F#**   **Em⁷**
A no-smoking sign on your cigarette break.
        D/F#   **Gsus²**
It's like ten thousand spoons
           D/F#   **Em⁷**
When all you need is a knife,
     D/F#   **Gsus²**
It's meeting the man of my dreams
         D/F#   **Em⁷**
And then meeting his beautiful wife.
        D/F# **Gsus²**   **D/F#**   **Em⁷**
And isn't it ironic? don't you think?
        D/F# **Gsus²**   **D/F#**   **Em⁷**
A little too ironic, and yeah, I really do think.

Chorus 3   As Chorus 1

     Cmaj⁷ D⁶ᐟ⁴   **Cmaj⁷**   **D⁶ᐟ⁴**

Outro   And you know life has a funny way of sneaking up on you,
     Cmaj⁷   **D⁶ᐟ⁴**   **Cmaj⁷**
Life has a funny, funny way of helping you out.

Helping you out.

RIGHT THROUGH YOU

Music by Alanis Morissette and Glenn Ballard ▪ Lyrics by Alanis Morissette

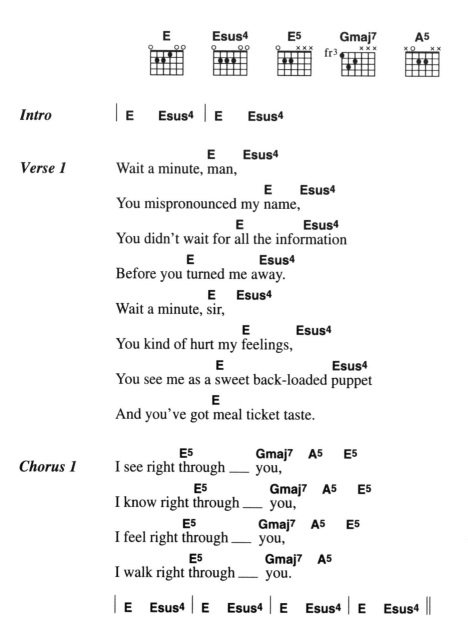

| | E | Esus4 | E5 | Gmaj7 | A5 |

Intro | E   Esus4 | E   Esus4

Verse 1

      E Esus4
Wait a minute, man,

        E Esus4
You mispronounced my name,

          E   Esus4
You didn't wait for all the information

      E   Esus4
Before you turned me away.

      E Esus4
Wait a minute, sir,

        E Esus4
You kind of hurt my feelings,

      E   Esus4
You see me as a sweet back-loaded puppet

      E
And you've got meal ticket taste.

Chorus 1

    E5   Gmaj7 A5 E5
I see right through __ you,

    E5   Gmaj7 A5 E5
I know right through __ you,

    E5   Gmaj7 A5 E5
I feel right through __ you,

    E5   Gmaj7 A5
I walk right through __ you.

| E   Esus4 | E   Esus4 | E   Esus4 | E   Esus4 ‖

Verse 2

                 E   **Esus⁴**
You took me for a joke,

                 E   **Esus⁴**
You took me for a child,

           E   **Esus⁴**
You took a long hard look at my ass

              E   **Esus⁴**
And then played golf for a while.

               E   **Esus⁴**
Your shake is like a fish,

               E   **Esus⁴**
You pat me on the head,

           E   **Esus⁴**
You took me out to wine, dine, sixty-nine me,

              E
But didn't hear a damn word I said.

Chorus 2   As Chorus 1

Verse 3

                 E   **Esus⁴**
Well, hello Mister Man,

               E   **Esus⁴**
You didn't think I'd come back,

               E   **Esus⁴**
You didn't think I'd show up with my army

           E   **Esus⁴**
And this ammunition on my back.

           E   **Esus⁴**
Now that I'm Miss Thing,

           E   **Esus⁴**
Now that I'm a zillionaire,

           E   **Esus⁴**
You scan the credits for your name

           E
And wonder why it's not there.

Chorus 3

         E⁵   **Gmaj⁷** **A⁵** **E⁵**
I see right through ___ you,

           E⁵   **Gmaj⁷** **A⁵** **E⁵**
I know right through ___ you,

           E⁵   **Gmaj⁷** **A⁵** **E⁵**
I feel right through ___ you,

           E⁵   **Gmaj⁷** **A⁵**
I walk right through ___ you.

GOODNIGHT GIRL

Words and Music by Graeme Clark, Tom Cunningham, Neil Mitchell & Marti Pellow

A   Dmaj7   Gmaj7   Bm7   Bm7/E   F#m   Dmaj9   Amaj7   Cmaj7

Verse 1

    A
You hear me so clearly

    Dmaj7
And see how I try.

    A
You feel me, so heal me

    Dmaj7
And tear me apart.

    Gmaj7
And I won't tell a soul,

     A
I won't tell at all.

    Gmaj7
And do they have to know

          Bm7
(Do they have to know)

  Bm7/E   **A**
About my goodnight girl?

Chorus 1

  (A)
Caught up in your wishing well,

       F#m
Your hopes inside it,

                    Bm7
Take your love and promises and make them last,

  Bm7/E
You make them last.

Verse 2

        A
You keep me so near you
     Dmaj7
And see me so far.
       A
And hold me and send me,
Dmaj7
Deep in your heart.
      Gmaj7
And I won't tell a soul,
       A
I won't tell at all.
      Gmaj7
And I won't let them know
            Bm7
(I won't let them know)
   Bm7/E   **A**
About my goodnight girl.

     (A)
Chorus 2   Caught up in your wishing well,
            F♯m
Your hopes inside it,
                     Bm7
Take your love and promises and make them last,
     Bm7/E
You make them last.

Chorus 3   As Chorus 2

     Dmaj9   **Amaj7**   **Dmaj9**
Middle   Doesn't matter how sad I made you,
               Amaj7   **Dmaj9**
Doesn't matter how hard I've tried.
           Amaj9
Just remember the same old reason
    Cmaj7
Reflected in your eyes, you said you wanted me.

Chorus 4   As Chorus 2

Chorus 5   As Chorus 2

LOVE IS ALL AROUND

Words and Music by Reg Presley

F   B♭/F   F7   B♭   Cm   E♭   Fsus4

Intro | F   B♭/F | F7   B♭/F | F   B♭/F | F7

Verse 1
B♭   Cm   E♭   F   B♭ Cm | E♭   F
I feel it in my fingers, I feel it in my toes,
B♭   Cm   E♭   F   B♭ Cm | E♭   F
The love that's all around me, and so the feeling grows,
B♭   Cm E♭   F   B♭ Cm | E♭   F
It's written on the wind, it's everywhere I go,
B♭   Cm   E♭   F   B♭ Cm | E♭ F | F   ‖ E♭
So if you really love me, come on and let it show.

Chorus 1
                          Cm   E♭
You know I love you, I always will,
                          B♭
My mind's made up by the way I feel.
          E♭   Cm
There's no beginning, there'll be no end,
                          F   F7
'Cause on my love you can depend.

Instrumental | B♭   Cm | E♭   Fsus4 F | B♭   Cm | E♭   Fsus4 F

Verse 2
B♭   Cm   E♭   F   B♭ Cm | E♭   F
I see your face before me as I lay on my bed,
B♭   Cm   E♭   F   B♭ Cm | E♭   F
I cannot get to thinking of all the things you said.
B♭   Cm E♭   F   B♭ Cm | E♭   F
You gave your promise to me and I gave mine to you,
B♭   Cm   E♭   F   B♭ Cm | E♭ F | F   ‖ E♭
I need someone beside me in everything I do.

Chorus 2

(E♭)   **Cm**   **E♭**
You know I love you, I always will,

              B♭
My mind's made up by the way I feel.

   E♭   **Cm**
There's no beginning, there'll be no end,

         F   **F7 B♭/F** | **F7 B♭/F** | **F**
'Cause on my love you can depend.

      B♭/F   **F7**
Got to keep it moving.

Verse 3

   B♭   **Cm E♭**   **Fsus4 F B♭ Cm** | **E♭ F**
It's written in the wind, oh, everywhere I go,

   B♭   **Cm E♭**   **Fsus4 F**   **B♭ Cm** | **E♭**
So if you really love me, come on and let it show,

     F
Come on and let it (show).

 B♭   **Cm**
‖: Come on and let it,

E♭   **Fsus4 F**
Come on and let   it,

B♭   **Cm E♭** **Fsus4 F**
Come on and let it show.   :‖ *Repeat to fade*

SWEET SURRENDER

Words and Music by Graeme Clark, Tom Cunningham, Neil Mitchell & Marti Pellow

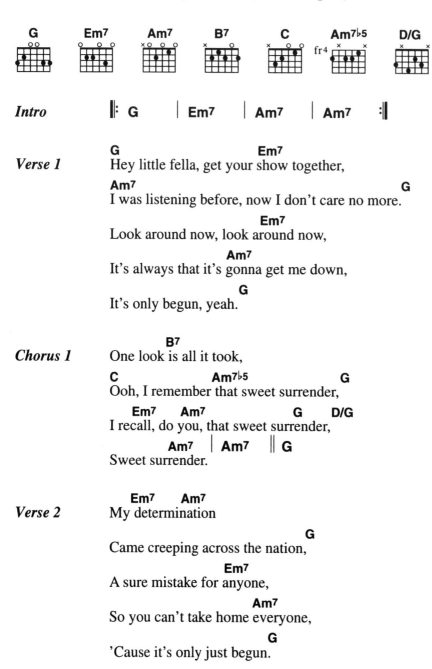

Intro

‖: G | Em7 | Am7 | Am7 :‖

Verse 1

G   Em7
Hey little fella, get your show together,

Am7   G
I was listening before, now I don't care no more.

         Em7
Look around now, look around now,

      Am7
It's always that it's gonna get me down,

      G
It's only begun, yeah.

Chorus 1

     B7
One look is all it took,

C   Am7♭5   G
Ooh, I remember that sweet surrender,

 Em7 Am7   G D/G
I recall, do you, that sweet surrender,

   Am7 | Am7 ‖ G
Sweet surrender.

Verse 2

  Em7 Am7
My determination

            G
Came creeping across the nation,

     Em7
A sure mistake for anyone,

       Am7
So you can't take home everyone,

       G
'Cause it's only just begun.

Chorus 2
```
(G)       B7                C
One look was all it took
            Am7♭5                    G
To remember that sweet surrender,
      Em7     Am7              G
I recall, do you, that sweet surrender.
```

Bridge 1
```
        Em7              Bm7
I don't know, I don't care,

'Cause I'm living without you baby,
B7                                C   Am7♭5
Even when I know what's going on, yeah, it only took
G          B7
One look, one glance,
C                          Am7♭5            G
Ooh, and it set my heart, set for romance.
          Em7      Am7     G     D/G
Do you believe my sweet surrender,
              Am/G
My sweet surrender?
```

Verse 3
```
G                        Em7
Hey little fella, now your show's together,
          Am7
I never wanted you to listen before,
                                G
So why should I walk out the door.
              Em7
Stick around now,
              Am7
And so the story goes on through the night,
            G
It's only begun.
```

Chorus 3
```
        B7              C
One look is all it took,
          Am7♭5                G
I remember that sweet surrender,
      Em7        Am7              G
Do you recall, 'cause I do, my sweet surrender.
```

Continued on next page...

Bridge 2

Em7   Bm7
I don't know, I don't care,

'Cause I'm living without you baby,

B7   C Am7♭5
Even when I know what's going on, yeah, it's all it takes

G   B7
One look, one glance.

C   Am7♭5   G
Ooh, and it set my heart, set for romance.

   Em7 Am7   G
One look is all it took, my sweet surrender,

D/G   Am/G G
My sweet surrender.

  (G)   D/G   Am/G G
‖: One look is all it took remember. :‖ *Repeat ad lib. to fade*

ODE TO MY FAMILY

Words and Music by Dolores O'Riordan & Noel Hogan

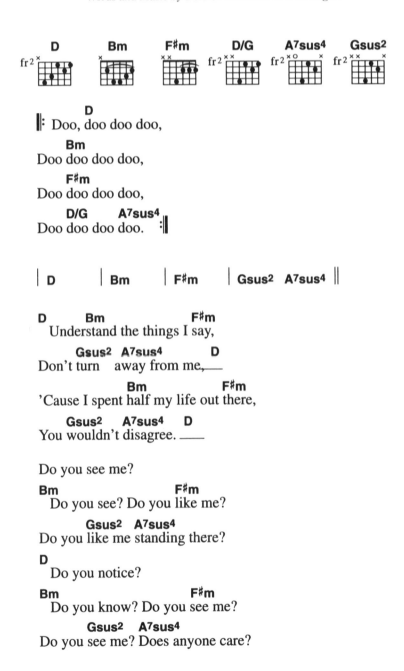

Intro

‖: Doo, doo doo doo, (D)

Doo doo doo doo, (Bm)

Doo doo doo doo, (F#m)

Doo doo doo doo. :‖ (D/G A7sus4)

| D | Bm | F#m | Gsus2 A7sus4 ‖

Verse 1

Understand the things I say, (D Bm F#m)

Don't turn   away from me, — (Gsus2 A7sus4 D)

'Cause I spent half my life out there, (Bm F#m)

You wouldn't disagree. —— (Gsus2 A7sus4 D)

Do you see me?

Do you see? Do you like me? (Bm F#m)

Do you like me standing there? (Gsus2 A7sus4)

Do you notice? (D)

Do you know? Do you see me? (Bm F#m)

Do you see me? Does anyone care? (Gsus2 A7sus4)

Chorus 1

    D   **Bm**   **F♯m**
    Unhappiness where's when I was young
        Gsus2   **A7sus4**   **D**
And we didn't give a damn, ____
             Bm
'Cause we were raised
        F♯m   **Gsus2** **A7sus4**   **D**
To see life as fun and take it if we can. ____
           Bm   **F♯m**
My mother, my mother she hold me,
    Gsus2   **A7sus4**
She hold me when I was out there.
D   **Bm**   **F♯m**
  My father, my father he liked me,
    Gsus2   **A7sus4**
Oh, he liked me. Does anyone care?

| **D** | **Bm** | **F♯m** | **Gsus2** **A7sus4** ‖

Verse 2

    D   **Bm**   **F♯m**
    Understand what I've become,
    Gsus2 **A7sus4**   **D**
It wasn't my design, ____
         Bm
And people ev'rywhere think
F♯m   **Gsus2** **A7sus4**   **D**
Something better than I am. ____
         Bm
I miss you,
         F♯m
I miss, 'cause I liked it,
     Gsus2 **A7sus4**
'Cause I liked it when I was out there.
D   **Bm**
  Do you know this?
                F♯m
Do you know you did not find me?
    Gsus2 **A7sus4**
You did not find, does anyone care?

Chorus 2

    D   Bm   F♯m
Unhappiness where's when I was young

          Gsus²   A⁷sus⁴   D
And we didn't give a damn, ____

               Bm
'Cause we were raised

        F♯m   Gsus² A⁷sus⁴   D
To see life as fun and take it if we can. ____

               Bm   F♯m
My mother, my mother she hold me,

      Gsus²   A⁷sus⁴
She hold me when I was out there.

D   Bm   F♯m
  My father, my father he liked me.

           Gsus²
Oh, he liked me.

        A⁷sus⁴   D
Does anyone care? ____

                    Bm
Does anyone care? ____

                    F♯m
Does anyone care? ____

                    Gsus²
Does anyone care? ____

        A⁷sus⁴   D
Does anyone care? ____

                    Bm
Does anyone care? ____

                    F♯m
Does anyone care? ____

                    Gsus² A⁷sus⁴
Does anyone care? ____

Outro

           D
‖: Doo, doo doo doo,

       Bm
Doo doo doo doo,

       F♯m
Doo doo doo doo,

       D/G   A⁷sus⁴
Doo doo doo doo   :‖ *Play 3 times*

| D | Bm | F♯m | D | ‖

NOT SORRY

Words by Dolores O'Riordan ▪ Music by Noel Hogan & Dolores O'Riordan

Am2 fr5 **C/F** **C** **G6** **G6/D** **Fmaj7** **Am**

Intro ‖: Am2 | C/F | C | G6 |

| Am2 | C/F | C | G6 :‖

Verse 1
   Am2   C/F
Keep on looking through the window again,
     C   G6/D
But I'm not sorry if I do insult you,
    Am2   C/F
I'm sad, not sorry, 'bout the way that things went,
     C   G6
And you'll be happy and I'll be forsakin' thee.

Verse 2
   Am2   C/F
I swore I'd never feel like this again,
     C   G6/D
But you're so selfish you don't see what you're doing to me,
   Am2   C/F
I keep on looking through the window again.
     C   G6   Am2
No, I'm not sorry If I do insult you, ___
   C/F   G6   Fmaj7
No, I'm not sorry if I do insult you. ___

Chorus 1

           Am
You told me lies and I sighed, and I sighed,

               Fmaj⁷
And I sighed, 'cause you lied,

         Am
Lied, and I cried, yes I cried,

           Fmaj⁷
Yes I cry, I cry, I try again.

   Am
I realise, as he sighed, and he sighed,

          Fmaj⁷
And he sighed 'cause you lied,

        Am
Lied and I cried, yes I cried,

Yes I cry, I cry, I try again.

Verse 3   As Verse 1

Verse 4

Am²   **C/F**
I swore I'd never feel like this again,

   C   **G⁶/D**
But you're so selfish you don't see what you're doing to me,

Am²   **C/F**
I keep on looking through the window again.

   C   **G⁶**   **Am²**
No, I'm not sorry if I do detest you, ⎯

   C/F   **G⁶**   **Fmaj⁷**
No, I'm not sorry if I do detest you. ⎯

Chorus 2   As Chorus 1

Outro

Am²   **C/F**   **C**   **G⁶/D**
Keep on looking through the window again,

Am²   **C/F**   **C**   **G⁶**
Keep on looking through the window again.

‖: **Am²** | **C/F** | **C** | **G⁶** :‖ **Am²** ‖

EVERYTHING I SAID

Words by Dolores O'Riordan ▪ Music by Dolores O'Riordan & Noel Hogan

Cmaj7   C   Em   C2/E   Fmaj9#11   Fmaj9

G6   G5/6   Fmaj7   Am   Em/B   G6*

Capo 3rd fret

Intro

| Cmaj7 | C Cmaj7 | Em | C2/E | |

| Fmaj9#11 | Fmaj9 | G6 | G5/6 G6 | |

Verse 1

Cmaj7   C   Cmaj7
It makes me lonely,____

Em   C2/E
It makes me very lonely

      Fmaj9#11   Fmaj9   G6   G5/6 G6
When I see you here,   waitin' on.

Cmaj7   C   Cmaj7
It makes me tired, ____

   Em   C2/E
It makes me very tired,

      Fmaj9#11   Fmaj9   G6   G5/6 G6
And inside of me,   lingers on.

Verse 2

       Cmaj7   C   Cmaj7
But you have your heart, oh,

      Em   C2/E
Don't believe it,____

      Fmaj9#11   Fmaj9   G6   G5/6 G6
And you ran outside,   waiting on. ____

      Cmaj7   C   Cmaj7
Ev'rything I said, oh,

      Em   C2/E
Well I meant it, ____

      Fmaj9#11   Fmaj9   G6   G5/6 G6
And inside my head,   holdin' on.

Bridge

Fmaj7   **Am**
'Cause if I died tonight,

                    Em/B
Would you hold my head, oh,

                              G6*
Would you understand? ____

Fmaj7   **Am**
  And if I lied in spite,

                       Em/B
Would you still be here, no,

                    G6*
Would you disappear?

Verse 3

Cmaj7 C   **Cmaj7 Em**
      Surely must be you,

C2/E   **Fmaj9#11**
Surely must be you,

      Fmaj9   **G6**   **G5/6 G6**
But I don't make you lonely,   la.

Cmaj7 C   **Cmaj7 Em**
      I'll get over   you,

C2/E   **Fmaj9#11**
I'll get over you,

      Fmaj9   **G6**   **G5/6 G6**
But I don't make you lonely,   la.

Outro

‖: **Cmaj7**   **Em**
   La, da, da, da, da, da.

C2/E   **Fmaj9#11**
La, da, da, da, da,

Fmaj9   **G6**   **G5/6 G6**
La, da, da, da, da, da, da,   la.   :‖

Cmaj7
  La, da, da, da, da, da,

La, da, da, da, da, da.

15 YEARS

Words & Music by Simon Friend, Charles Heather, Mark Chadwick, Jonathon Sevink & Jeremy Cunningham

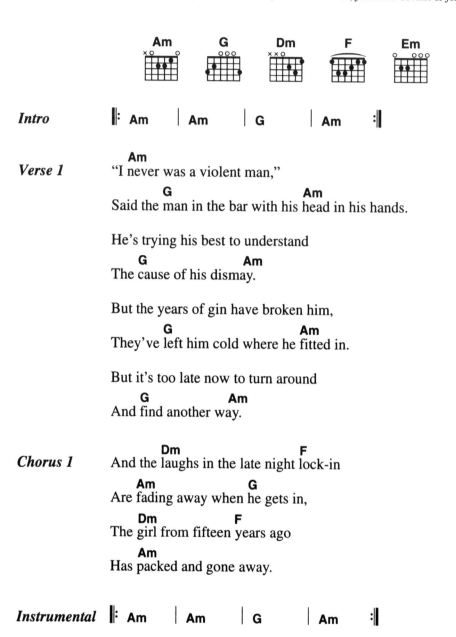

Intro   ‖: Am | Am | G | Am :‖

Verse 1

Am
"I never was a violent man,"
     G   Am
Said the man in the bar with his head in his hands.

He's trying his best to understand
     G   Am
The cause of his dismay.

But the years of gin have broken him,
     G   Am
They've left him cold where he fitted in.

But it's too late now to turn around
     G   Am
And find another way.

Chorus 1

          Dm   F
And the laughs in the late night lock-in
  Am   G
Are fading away when he gets in,
  Dm   F
The girl from fifteen years ago
  Am
Has packed and gone away.

Instrumental   ‖: Am | Am | G | Am :‖

Verse 2

        Am
"That's never how it used to be,

    G   **Am**
What happened to all that energy?

You took one too many liberties,

    G   **Am**
I'm tired of being afraid."

So the night after the fight she took flight,

    G   **Am**
Hiding swollen eyes and a wounded pride,

The best years of her life denied

    G   **Am**
And sold for liquid shares.

Chorus 2   As Chorus 1

Middle

(Am)   **Em** **C**   **G**
And the victims of their world are advertised on posters,

    Am   **Em** **C**   **G**
Just a beach and a pretty girl   if you take this potion.

Verse 3

    Am
It's another week till his cheque comes through,

    G   **Am**
He's got a fiver left now to spend on food,

But the doors of the bar are open,

    G   **Am**
And he breaks another rule.

Well he sits on a stool that bears his name,

    G   **Am**
He's got a favourite glass that's called the same,

He's never been kept waiting

    G   **Am**
'Cos he pays the landlord's wage.

Chorus 3   As Chorus 1

Chorus 4   As Chorus 1

C.C.T.V.

Words & Music by Simon Friend, Charles Heather, Mark Chadwick, Jonathon Sevink & Jeremy Cunningham

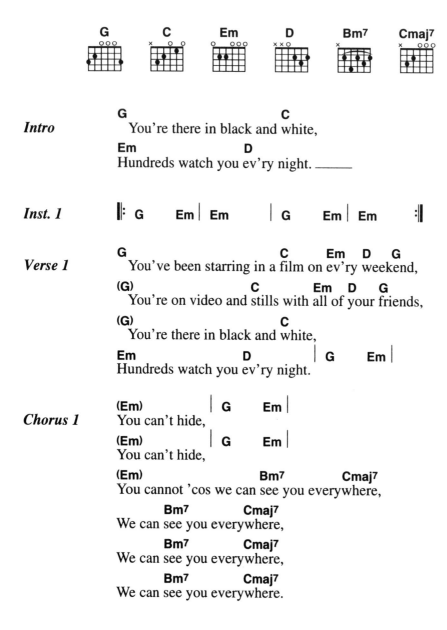

Intro

G   C
You're there in black and white,
Em   D
Hundreds watch you ev'ry night. _____

Inst. 1 ‖: G Em | Em | G Em | Em   :‖

Verse 1

G   C Em D G
You've been starring in a film on ev'ry weekend,
(G)   C   Em D G
You're on video and stills with all of your friends,
(G)   C
You're there in black and white,
Em   D | G Em |
Hundreds watch you ev'ry night.

Chorus 1

(Em) | G Em |
You can't hide,
(Em) | G Em |
You can't hide,
(Em)   Bm7   Cmaj7
You cannot 'cos we can see you everywhere,
   Bm7   Cmaj7
We can see you everywhere,
   Bm7   Cmaj7
We can see you everywhere,
   Bm7   Cmaj7
We can see you everywhere.

Verse 2

    G   C   Em D G
You're great in every scene, you're very natural,

    (G)   C   Em   D G
It's as if you cannot see the spotlight on you,

    (G)   C
But when you fluff a line

        Em   D | G   Em |
The director says you're doing time.

Chorus 2   As Chorus 1

Middle

    G   A
When you're walking home

      D   G
In the evenin' after dark,

    Em   G   Em   G
Remember don't hide and show your best side

         D   C
'Cos you're a star in a film.

Inst. 2   ‖: G   Em | Em | G   Em | Em   :‖ G   Em |

    (Em) | G   Em |
You can't hide.

    (Em) | G   Em ‖
You can't hide.

Chorus 3   As Chorus 1

    | G   Em | Em   ‖

BELARUSE

Words & Music by Simon Friend, Charles Heather, Mark Chadwick, Jonathon Sevink & Jeremy Cunningham

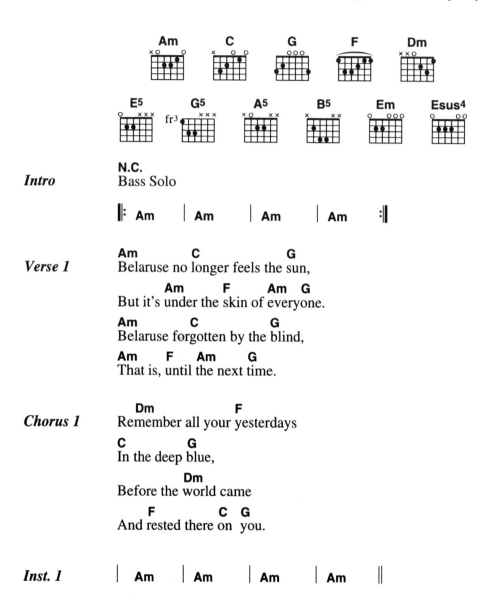

Intro

N.C.
Bass Solo

‖: Am | Am | Am | Am :‖

Verse 1

Am   C   G
Belaruse no longer feels the sun,

    Am F Am G
But it's under the skin of everyone.

Am   C   G
Belaruse forgotten by the blind,

Am F Am   G
That is, until the next time.

Chorus 1

    Dm   F
Remember all your yesterdays

C   G
In the deep blue,

      Dm
Before the world came

    F   C G
And rested there on you.

Inst. 1 | Am | Am | Am | Am ‖

Verse 1

        Am   **C**   **G**
And if the sun and moon were both to doubt,

Am   **F**   **Am**   **G**
Sure enough they'd both go out.

                Am   **C**   **G**
When you can't walk in your field, feel water in your hands,

Am   **F**   **Am**   **G**
You've been touched by the doubt of man.

Chorus 2

      Dm   **F**
Remember all your yesterdays

C   **G**
In the deep blue,

         Dm
Before the world came

     F   **C G**
And rested there on you.

Inst. 2

‖: E5 G5 E5 G5 | E5 A5 E5 A5 |

| E5 B5 E5 B5 | B5 A5 G5   :‖ *Play 3 times*

‖: Em   Esus4 | Em   Esus4 :‖

| E5 G5 E5 G5 | E5 A5 E5 A5 | E5 B5 E5 B5 | B5 A5 G5   ‖

Chorus 3

      Dm   **F**
Remember all your yesterdays

C   **G**
In the deep blue,

         Dm
Before the world came

     F   **C G**
And rested there on you.

Outro

N.C.
Bass Solo

‖: E5 G5 E5 G5 | E5 A5 E5 A5 |

| E5 B5 E5 B5 | B5 A5 G5   :‖ *Play 4 times*

| E5   ‖

MADE OF STONE

Words & Music by Ian Brown & John Squire

Em⁷ Em⁶ Cmaj⁷/E *Em Em D C B G

Intro   ‖: Em⁷ | Em⁶ | Cmaj⁷/E | *Em :‖

Verse 1

Em   D
Your knuckles whiten on the wheel,

                                    C
The last thing that your hands will feel,

                              B
Your final flight can't be delayed.

Em   D
No earth, just sky it's so serene,

                              C
Your pink fat lips let go a scream,

                              B
You fry and melt, I love the scene.

Chorus 1

                    G   D   C
Sometimes I fantasize when the streets are cold and lonely

            G
And the cars they burn below me.

                              D   C
Don't these times fill your eyes when the streets are cold and lonely

            G
And the cars they burn below me,

            D   Em
Are you alone, is anybody home?

Link | Em | Em | D | D |

            | C | C | B | B   ‖

Verse 2

Em   D
I'm standing warm against the cold,

                                  C
Now that the flames have taken hold

                            B
At least you left your life in style.

Em   D
And for as far as I can see,

                              C
Ten twisted grilles grin back at me,

                         B
Bad money dies, I love the scene.

Chorus 2   As Chorus 1

Solo

| Em | Em | D | D | |
| C | C | B | B | :‖ *Play 3 times* |

Chorus 3

                 G   D   C
Sometimes I fantasize when the streets are cold and lonely

             G
And the cars they burn below me.

                      D   C
Don't these times fill your eyes when the streets are cold and lonely.

             G
And the cars they burn below me,

             D   Em
Are you alone, are you made of stone?

Outro

| ‖: Em7 | Em6 | Cmaj7/E | *Em | :‖ |

SHE BANGS THE DRUMS

Words & Music by Ian Brown & John Squire

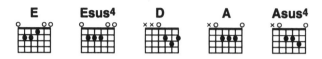

Intro   ‖: E | E   Esus⁴ :‖

Verse 1

E   Esus⁴ E
I can feel the earth begin to move,
                    Esus⁴ D
I hear my needle hit the groove.

And spiral through another day,
                              E
I hear my song begin to say:
                    Esus⁴   E
"Kiss me where the sun don't shine,
                         Esus⁴ D
The past was yours but the future's mine,

You're all out of time."

Verse 2

E   Esus⁴ E
I don't feel too steady on my feet,
               Esus⁴ D
I feel hollow, I feel   weak.

Passion fruit and Holy bread
                              E
Fill my guts and ease my head.
                    Esus⁴   E
Through the early morning sun
               Esus⁴ D
I can see her, here she comes,

She bangs the drums.

Chorus 1

```
A          D              A
Have you seen her, have you heard?
            D              A
The way she plays, there are no words
            D          E
To describe the way I feel.
A          D          A
How could it ever come to pass?
            D          A
She'll be the first, she'll be the last
            D          E
To describe the way I feel, the way I feel.
```

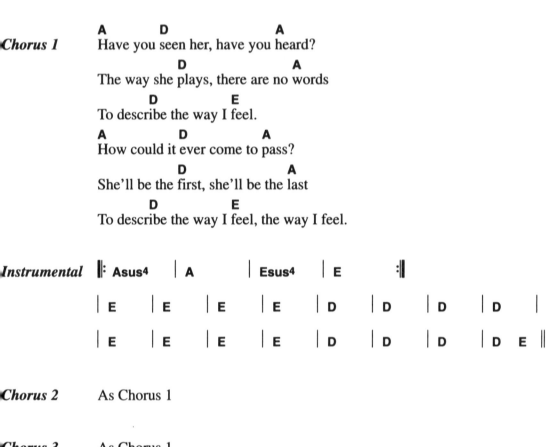

```
Instrumental  ‖: Asus4  | A       | Esus4  | E        :‖

              | E    | E    | E    | E    | D    | D    | D    | D    |

              | E    | E    | E    | E    | D    | D    | D    | D  E ‖
```

Chorus 2   As Chorus 1

Chorus 3   As Chorus 1

Outro   *Instrumental as Chorus to fade*

WHAT THE WORLD IS WAITING FOR

Words & Music by Ian Brown & John Squire

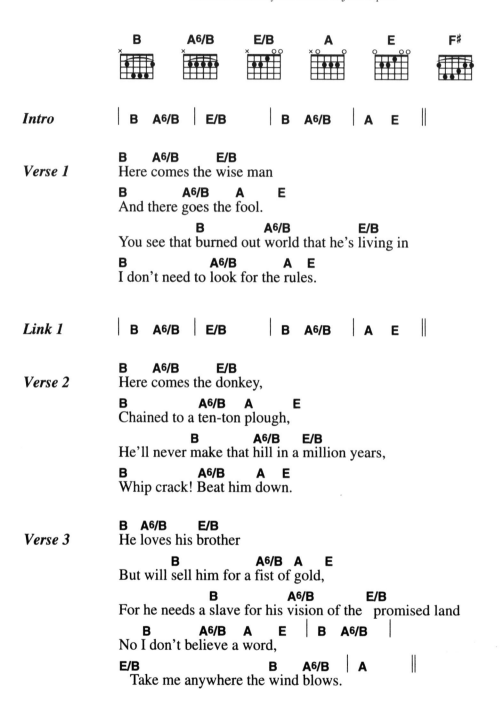

Intro | B A6/B | E/B | B A6/B | A E ||

Verse 1
B   A6/B   E/B
Here comes the wise man
B   A6/B   A   E
And there goes the fool.
          B   A6/B   E/B
You see that burned out world that he's living in
B   A6/B   A E
I don't need to look for the rules.

Link 1 | B A6/B | E/B | B A6/B | A E ||

Verse 2
B   A6/B   E/B
Here comes the donkey,
B   A6/B A   E
Chained to a ten-ton plough,
          B   A6/B E/B
He'll never make that hill in a million years,
B   A6/B   A E
Whip crack! Beat him down.

Verse 3
B A6/B   E/B
He loves his brother
          B   A6/B A   E
But will sell him for a fist of gold,
              B   A6/B   E/B
For he needs a slave for his vision of the   promised land
      B   A6/B   A   E | B A6/B |
No I don't believe a word,
E/B   B A6/B | A ||
    Take me anywhere the wind blows.

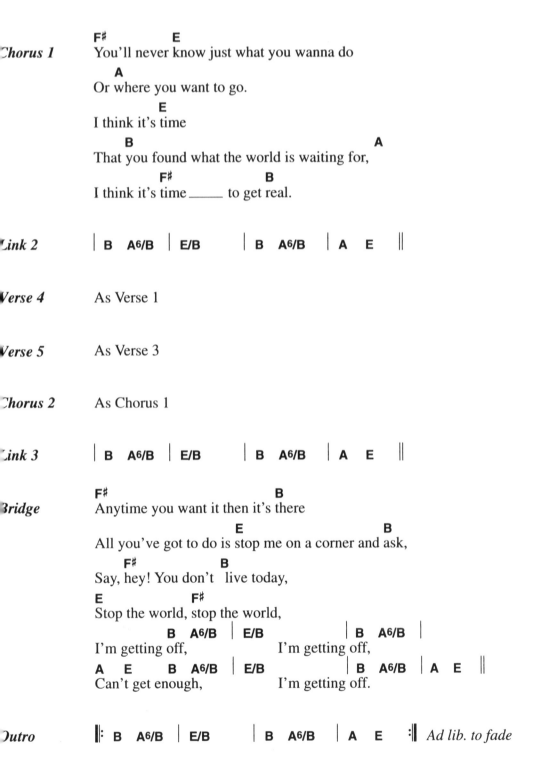

Chorus 1

F#   E
You'll never know just what you wanna do
   A
Or where you want to go.
        E
I think it's time
    B   A
That you found what the world is waiting for,
        F#   B
I think it's time _____ to get real.

Link 2
| B A6/B | E/B | B A6/B | A E ||

Verse 4   As Verse 1

Verse 5   As Verse 3

Chorus 2   As Chorus 1

Link 3
| B A6/B | E/B | B A6/B | A E ||

Bridge

F#   B
Anytime you want it then it's there
                     E   B
All you've got to do is stop me on a corner and ask,
     F#   B
Say, hey! You don't   live today,
E   F#
Stop the world, stop the world,
              B A6/B | E/B | B A6/B |
I'm getting off,   I'm getting off,
A E   B A6/B | E/B | B A6/B | A E ||
Can't get enough,   I'm getting off.

Outro
||: B A6/B | E/B | B A6/B | A E :|| *Ad lib. to fade*

BULL-RUSH

Words & Music by Paul Weller

[Chord diagrams: E D C#m Bm7 Dsus2 Em7 A]

[Chord diagrams: Esus4 Asus4 G5 Am/D Gm7/C Fm7/B♭ Dm7/11 A11]

Intro | E | D | C#m | Bm7 | E | D | E | D ||

Verse 1

E   D   Dsus2
In a momentary lapse of my condition,

E   D   Dsus2
Sent me tumbling down into a deep despair,

E   D   Dsus2
Lost and dazed so I had no real recollection,

Em7   A   E   Esus4
Until the rain cleared the air.

Verse 2

E   D   Dsus2
When you wake to find that everything has left you,

E   D   Dsus2
And the clothes you wear belong to someone else,

E   D   Dsus2
See your shadow chasing off towards the shore line,

Em7   A   E
Drifting into emptiness.

Chorus 1

          D   Dsus2 E   Esus4 E
There are bull rushes outside my window,

          Asus4   A   E   Esus4 E
And their leaves whisper words in the breeze,

       D   Dsus2 E
Well tomorrow I'll walk to the harbour,

        G5   A   E   Esus4
Catch the first boat that's coming in,

E   G5   A   E   Esus4 E
I'll catch the first boat that's coming in.

Verse 3

(E)   D   Dsus2
Like a child too small to reach the front door handle,

E   D   Dsus2
Or maybe just too scared to know what I would find,

E   D   Dsus2
Now I feel I'm strong enough to take the slow ride

Em7   A   E   Esus4   E
Not knowing when I will arrive.

Chorus 2   As Chorus 1

Middle

D   E
I do believe I'm going home,

D   E
'Cause I don't call this place my own,

Bm7   A
I'm missing what I had,

Am/D   Gm7/C
Happy times and sad,

         Fm7/B♭
More than I ever thought could be.

Instrumental | Dm7/11 | A11 | Dm7/11 | A11 ||

E   D
La la la la la la la la la la la la,

E   D
La la la la la la la la la la la,

E   D
La la la la la la la la la la la,

Em7   A   E
Not knowing when I will arrive.

Chorus 3   As Chorus 1

Outro

E   G5   A   E   Esus4
I'll catch the first boat that's coming in, yeah,

G5 A   G5 A   G5 A   E
Yeah,   yeah,   that's coming in.

Instrumental ||: E | D   Dsus2 | E | D   Dsus2 :|| *Play 4 times*

||: E   D E | E   D E | E   D E | E   D E :|| *Repeat to fade*

YOU DO SOMETHING TO ME

Words & Music by Paul Weller

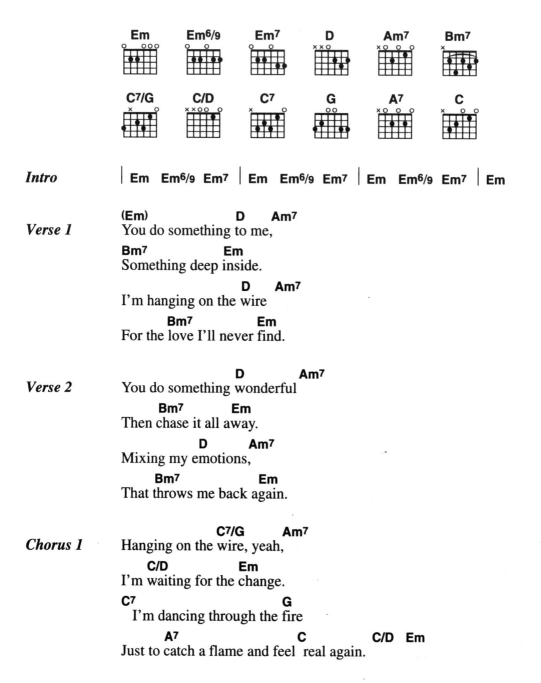

Intro | Em Em6/9 Em7 | Em Em6/9 Em7 | Em Em6/9 Em7 | Em ‖

Verse 1
(Em)   **D**   **Am7**
You do something to me,

Bm7   **Em**
Something deep inside.

               D   **Am7**
I'm hanging on the wire

       Bm7   **Em**
For the love I'll never find.

Verse 2
               D   **Am7**
You do something wonderful

   Bm7   **Em**
Then chase it all away.

          D   **Am7**
Mixing my emotions,

   Bm7   **Em**
That throws me back again.

Chorus 1
               C7/G   **Am7**
Hanging on the wire, yeah,

  C/D   **Em**
I'm waiting for the change.

C7   **G**
  I'm dancing through the fire

     A7   **C**   **C/D Em**
Just to catch a flame and feel real again.

Guitar solo   ‖: D | Am7 Bm7 | Em | Em   :‖

Chorus 2   As Chorus 1

                 (Em)   D   Am7
Verse 3   ·   You do something to me,
                 Bm7   Em
                 Somewhere deep inside.
                                  D   Am7
                 I'm hoping to get close to
                   Bm7   Em
                 A peace I cannot find.

                                  C7/G   Am7
Chorus 3   Dancing through the fire, yeah,
                 C/D   Em
                 Just to catch a flame.
                 C7   G
                   Just to get close to,
                   A7   C7   C/D Em
                 Just close enough to tell you that:
                                  D   Am7
                 You do something to me,
                 Bm7   Em   Em6/9 Em7
                   Something deep inside.

                 | Em   Em6/9 Em7 | Em   Em6/9 Em7 | Em   Em6/9 Em7 | Em   ‖

BAR ITALIA

Music by Pulp ▪ Lyrics by Jarvis Cocker

C   E   Am   F   Fm   B♭

Intro | C | C ‖

Verse 1

```
     C                E
   Now if you can stand,
       Am              F
   I would like to take you by the hand, yeah,
   C              E
   And go for a walk,
       Am          F
   Past people as they go to work.
   C                    E
   Let's get out of this place before
       Am                 Fm
   They tell us that we've just died, oh.
```

Chorus 1

```
   C                         E
   Move, move quick, you've gotta move,
       Am                    Fm
   Come on it's through, come on it's time,
           C                    E
   Oh, look at you, you're looking so confused,
           Am Fm
   Just what did you lose, oh.
```

| C | C ‖

Verse 2

 C   E
If you can make
  Am   F
An order, could you get me one?
 C   E
Two sugars would be great
   Am   F
'Cos I'm fading fast and it's nearly dawn.
 C   E
If they knocked down this place, this place,
   Am   Fm
It'd still look much better than you, oh now.

Chorus 2 As Chorus 1

 C
It's O.K. it's just your mind.

Instrumental ‖: C | E | Am | Fm :‖

 C   E
If we get through this ali-hi-hive,
   Am   Fm
I'll meet you next week, same place, same time, oh.

Chorus 3 As Chorus 1

     C
Outro That's what you get from clubbing it,
    E
You can't go home and go to bed
  Am
Because it hasn't worn off yet,
  Fm
And now it's morning.
   C
There's only one place we can go,
  E
It's around the corner in Soho
   Am   Fm
Where other broken people go.
B♭ C
Let's go.

MIS-SHAPES

Music by Pulp ▪ Lyrics by Jarvis Cocker

Verse 1

A
Mis-shapes, mistakes, misfits,

E　　　　　　　　　　　　　　　　　**Fm**
Raised on a diet of broken biscuits, oh,

F#m
　We don't look the same as you,

Dmaj7
　And we don't do the things you do,

　　D7
But we live 'round here too, oh really.

Verse 2

A
Mis-shapes, mistakes, misfits,

　　　E　　　　　　　　　　　　　　　　**Fm**
We'd like to go to town but we can't risk it, oh,

F#m
　'Cause they just want to keep us out,

Dmaj7
　You could end up with a smack in the mouth

D7
Just for standing out, now really.

A　　　　　　　　　**E7**
　Brother, sisters, can't you see

　　　　　　　　E　　　　　**Fm F#m**
The future's owned by you and me?

　　　　　　　　　　　　Dmaj7
There won't be fighting in the street,

They think they've got us beat,

　　D7　　　　　　　　　　　　　　　**G**
But revenge is going to be so sweet, oh. _____

Chorus 1

(G)   **Gaug**   **G6**
We're making a move, we're making it now,

      G7
We're coming out of the sidelines.

C   **Caug**   **C6**
 Just put your hands up, it's a raid, yeah.

C7   **Em**   **C/E**
 We want your homes, we want your lives,

     Em6   **C/E**
We want the things you won't allow us,

     Em   **C/E**
We won't use guns, we won't use bombs,

     Em6   **C/E**
We'll use the one thing we've got more of,

    Em
That's our minds.

Verse 3

    A
Check your lucky numbers,

E   **Fm**
That much money could drag you under, oh,

F♯m
 What's the point of being rich

Dmaj7
If you can't think what to do with it,

   D7
'Cause you're so bleeding thick.

 A   **E7**
 Oh, we weren't supposed to be,

     E
We learnt too much at school,

Fm **F♯m**
Now we can't help but see

   Dmaj7
The future that you've got mapped out

 D7   **G**
Is nothing much to shout about, oh. ‗‗‗

Chorus 2   As Chorus 1

Instrumental | **E** | **E** ||

      | **A** | **A** | **E** | **E** **Fm** | **F♯m** |

      | **F♯m** | **Dmaj7** | **Dmaj7** | **D7** | **D7** ||

Verse 4

              A   **E7**
And brother, sisters, can't you see

               E   **Fm F♯m**
The future's owned by you and me?

                            Dmaj7
There won't be fighting in the street,

They think that they've got us beat,

   D7   **G**
But revenge is going to be so sweet.

Chorus 2

                 Gaug   **G6**
We're making a move, we're making it now,

               G7
We're coming out of the sidelines.

C   **Caug**   **C6**
  Just put your hands up, it's a raid, yeah.

C7   **Em**   **C/E**
  We want your homes, we want your lives,

          Em6   **C/E**
We want the things you won't allow us,

          Em   **C/E**
We won't use guns, we won't use bombs,

          Em6   **C/E**
We'll use the one thing we've got more of,

         Em   **C/E**   **Em6**   **C/E**
That's our minds, _____ yeah.

           Em   **C/E**   **Em6**   **C/E**   **A**
And that's our minds, _____ yeah.

THE BEST GUITAR CHORD
SONGBOOK EVER!

CONTENTS

ALWAYS

Words and Music by Jon Bon Jovi

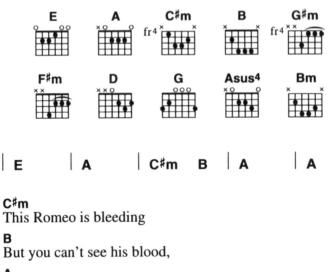

Intro | E | A | C#m B | A | A |

Verse 1

C#m
This Romeo is bleeding

B
But you can't see his blood,

A
It's nothing but some feeling

        G#m
That this old dog kicked up.

C#m
It's been raining since you left me,

        B
Now I'm drowning in the flood,

A
You see I've always been a fighter,

       G#m   A B
But without you I give up.

C#m
Now I can't sing a love song

       B
Like the way it's meant to be,

     A
Well I guess I'm not that good anymore,

    B   A B
But baby that's just me.

Chorus 1
    E   B   F♯m C♯m B
Yeah I will love you, baby, always.
    E   B   A C♯m B
And I'll be there forever and a day, always.

Bridge 1
E
I'll be there till the stars don't shine,
    B
Till the heavens burst and the words don't rhyme,
    A
I know when I die you'll be on my mind,
    B   A B C♯m A
And I'll love you always.

Verse 2
              C♯m
Now your pictures that you left behind
    B
Are just memories of a different life,
    A
Some that made us laugh, some that made us cry,
    G♯m
One that made you say goodbye.
    C♯m
What I'd give to run my fingers through your hair,
  B
To touch your lips, to hold you near,
    A
When you say your prayers, try to understand
   G♯m   A   B
I've made mistakes, I'm just a man.
    C♯m
When he holds you close, when he pulls you near,
   B
When he says the words you've been needing to hear,
   A
I'll wish I was him, 'cause the words are mine
  B   A   B
To say to you till the end of time.

Chorus 2   As Chorus 1

Continued on next page...

Bridge 2

   D   G   Asus⁴ A D
If you told me to cry for you, I could,

         G   Asus⁴ A Bm
If you told me to die for you, I would,

        G
Take a look at my face,

        A
There's no price I won't pay

To say these words to you.

Guitar solo | E | B | F♯m | C♯m B |

       | E | B | A | B A B |

        A
Well there ain't no luck in these loaded dice,

  B
But baby if you give me just one more try,

   A
We can pack up our old dreams and our old lives,

  B   A B
We'll find a place where the sun still shines.

Chorus 3 As Chorus 1

Bridge 3

   E
I'll be there till the stars don't shine,

   B
Till the heavens burst and the words don't rhyme,

   A
I know when I die you'll be on my mind,

  B A B
And I'll love you always.

Ad lib. solo ‖: E | B | C♯m B | A :‖ *Repeat to fade*

149

BED OF ROSES

Words and Music by Jon Bon Jovi

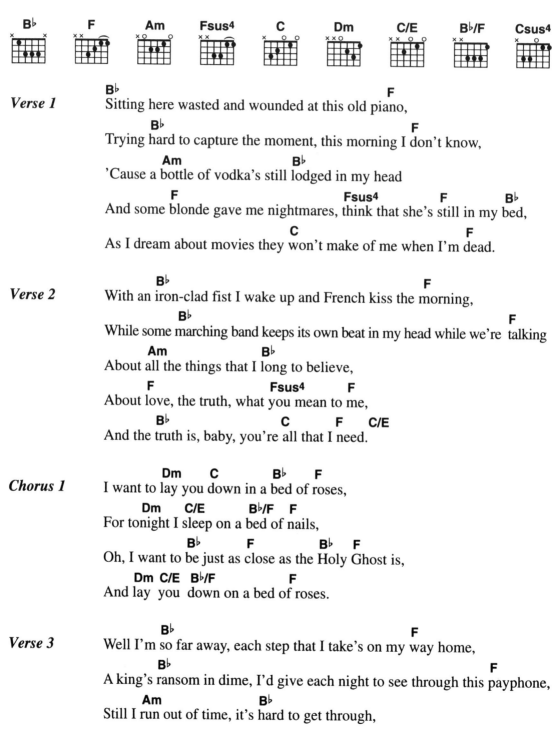

Verse 1

      B♭   F
Sitting here wasted and wounded at this old piano,

        B♭   F
Trying hard to capture the moment, this morning I don't know,

       Am   B♭
'Cause a bottle of vodka's still lodged in my head

          F   Fsus4   F   B♭
And some blonde gave me nightmares, think that she's still in my bed,

                        C   F
As I dream about movies they won't make of me when I'm dead.

Verse 2

       B♭   F
With an iron-clad fist I wake up and French kiss the morning,

       B♭   F
While some marching band keeps its own beat in my head while we're talking

       Am   B♭
About all the things that I long to believe,

       F   Fsus4   F
About love, the truth, what you mean to me,

       B♭   C   F   C/E
And the truth is, baby, you're all that I need.

Chorus 1

          Dm   C   B♭   F
I want to lay you down in a bed of roses,

          Dm   C/E   B♭/F F
For tonight I sleep on a bed of nails,

               B♭   F   B♭ F
Oh, I want to be just as close as the Holy Ghost is,

          Dm C/E B♭/F   F
And lay you down on a bed of roses.

Verse 3

       B♭   F
Well I'm so far away, each step that I take's on my way home,

       B♭   F
A king's ransom in dime, I'd give each night to see through this payphone,

       Am   B♭
Still I run out of time, it's hard to get through,

```
              F                       Fsus4      F
Till the bird on the wire flies me back to you,
    B♭                                          C          F      C/E
I'll just close my eyes and whisper, baby, blind love is true.
```

Chorus 2

```
          Dm      C           B♭    F
I want to lay you down in a bed of roses,
      Dm     C/E        B♭/F  F
For tonight I sleep on a bed of nails,
             B♭        F          B♭   F
Oh, I want to be just as close as the Holy Ghost is,
    Dm C/E  B♭/F        F       C/E
And lay you down on a bed of roses.
```

Middle

```
          B♭                   Csus4        C
Well this hotel bar's hangover, whiskey's gone dry,
         F
The bar keeper's wig's crooked and she's giving me the eye,
     B♭
Well I might have said "Yeah",
                      C       F      C/E
But I laughed so hard I think I died.
```

Guitar solo

```
| Dm   C  B♭ | F     | Dm   C/E  B♭/F | F     |
| Dm   C  B♭ | F     | Dm   C/E  B♭/F | F     |
```

Verse 4

```
        B♭                                     F
Now as you close your eyes, know I'll be thinking about you,
         B♭                                        F
While my mistress, she calls me to stand in her spotlight again,
         B♭                                           F
Tonight, I won't be alone, you know that don't mean I'm not lonely,
       Dm        C/E         B♭/F          F    C/E
I've got nothing to prove for it's you I'd die to defend.
```

Chorus 3

```
          Dm      C           B♭    F
I want to lay you down in a bed of roses,
      Dm     C/E        B♭/F  F
For tonight I sleep on a bed of nails,
             B♭        F          B♭   F
Oh, I want to be just as close as the Holy Ghost is,
    Dm C/E  B♭/F   F   C/E
And lay you down.
```

Chorus 4 As Chorus 1

YOU GIVE LOVE A BAD NAME

Words and Music by Jon Bon Jovi, Richie Sambora and Desmond Child.

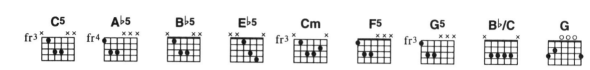

N.C.
Shot through the heart and you're to blame,
N.C.
Darlin' you give love a bad name.

Instrumental | C5 A♭5 | B♭5 C5 | A♭5 B♭5 | E♭5 C5 | C5 A♭5 | B♭5 C5 |
| A♭5 B♭5 | B♭5 | Cm(riff) |

Verse 1
      Cm
The angel's smile is what you sell,

You promise me heaven then put me through hell.

The chains of love got a hold on me,

When passion's a prison, you can't break free.
F5   **Cm**
Oh, you're a loaded gun, yeah,
B♭5
Oh, there's nowhere to run,
F5   **G5**
No one can save me, the damage is done.

Chorus 1
   C5   **A♭5**   **B♭5**   **C5**
Shot through the heart and you're to blame,
A♭5   **B♭5**   **E♭5 C5**
You give love a bad name (bad name).
   C5   **A♭5**   **B♭5**   **C5**
I play my part and you play your game,
A♭5   **B♭5**   **E♭5 C5**
You give love a bad name (bad name),
      A♭5   **B♭5**   **Cm B♭/C Cm**
Yeah, you give love a bad name.

Verse 2

Cm
Paint your smile on your lips,

Blood red nails on your fingertips.

A schoolboy's dream, you act so shy,

Your very first kiss was your first kiss goodbye.

F5   Cm
Oh, you're a loaded gun,

B♭5
Oh, there's nowhere to run,

F5   G
No one can save me, the damage is done.

Chorus 2

C5   A♭5   B♭5   C5
Shot through the heart and you're to blame,

A♭5   B♭5   E♭5 C5
You give love a bad name (bad name).

C5   A♭5   B♭5   C5
I play my part and you play your game,

A♭5   B♭5   E♭5 C5
You give love a bad name (bad name),

A♭5   B♭5
Yeah, you give love.

Play 3 times

Guitar solo ‖: C5 A♭5 | B♭5 C5 :‖ C5 A♭5 | G | G |

Chorus 3

C5   A♭5   B♭5   C5
Shot through the heart and you're to blame,

A♭5   B♭5   C5
You give love a bad name (bad name).

  C5   A♭5   B♭5   C5
I play my part and you play your game,

A♭5   B♭5   E♭5 C5
You give love a bad name (bad name).

Chorus 4   As Chorus 3

A♭5   B♭5 E♭5
You give love, oh, oh, oh,

A♭5   B♭5 E♭5 C5
You give love a bad name.

Repeat to fade

KEEP THE FAITH

Words and Music by Jon Bon Jovi, Richie Sambora and Desmond Child

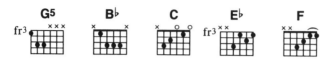

Verse 1

     G5   **B♭**
Mother, mother, tell your children
    C   **B♭ G5**
That their time has just begun,
    G5   **B♭**
I have suffered for my anger,
     C   **E♭** **F**
There are wars that can't be won.
    G5   **B♭**
Father, father, please believe me
   C   **B♭ G5**
I am laying down my guns,
   G5   **B♭**
I am broken like an arrow
    C **E♭**   **F**
Forgive me, forgive your wayward son.
G5   **B♭**
Everybody needs somebody to love,
C   **G5**
Everybody needs somebody to hate,
         B♭
Everybody's bitchin' 'cause they can't get enough,
   C   **E♭** **F**
It is hard to hold on when there's no-one to lean on.

Chorus 1

G5   **B♭**   **F**
Faith, you know you're gonna live through the rain,
  C   **G5**
Lord we've gotta keep the faith.
  B♭   **F**
Faith, don't you let your love turn to hate,
C   **G5**
Now we've gotta keep the faith,

Keep the faith, keep the faith,
      G5 | **B♭** | **C** **B♭**| **G5**
Lord we've gotta keep the faith.

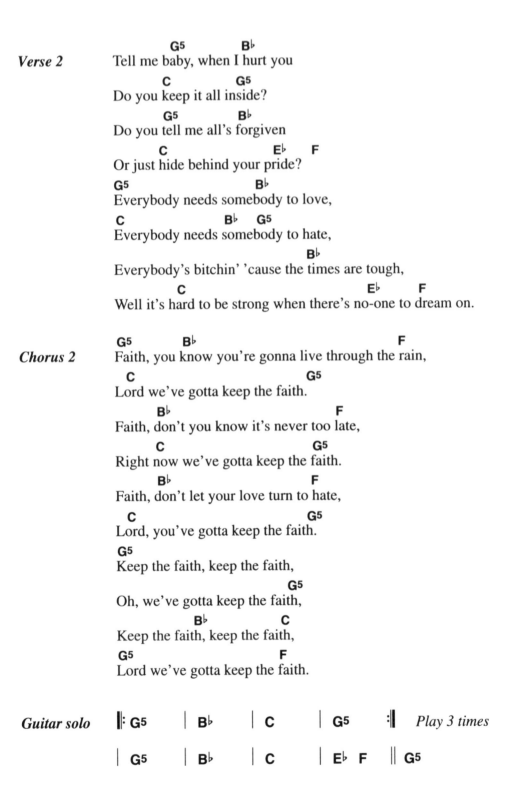

Verse 2

        G5   B♭
Tell me baby, when I hurt you

       C   G5
Do you keep it all inside?

       G5   B♭
Do you tell me all's forgiven

        C   E♭   F
Or just hide behind your pride?

G5   B♭
Everybody needs somebody to love,

C   B♭   G5
Everybody needs somebody to hate,

                   B♭
Everybody's bitchin' 'cause the times are tough,

         C   E♭   F
Well it's hard to be strong when there's no-one to dream on.

Chorus 2

G5   B♭   F
Faith, you know you're gonna live through the rain,

   C   G5
Lord we've gotta keep the faith.

     B♭   F
Faith, don't you know it's never too late,

      C   G5
Right now we've gotta keep the faith.

     B♭   F
Faith, don't let your love turn to hate,

   C   G5
Lord, you've gotta keep the faith.

G5
Keep the faith, keep the faith,

                      G5
Oh, we've gotta keep the faith,

        B♭   C
Keep the faith, keep the faith,

G5   F
Lord we've gotta keep the faith.

Guitar solo   ‖: G5 | B♭ | C | G5   :‖   *Play 3 times*

                    | G5 | B♭ | C | E♭ F ‖ G5

Continued on next page...

Spoken I've been walking in the footseps of society's lies,

I don't like what I see no more, sometimes I wish I was blind.

Sometimes I wait forever, to stand out in the rain,

So no-one sees me cryin', tryin' to wash away this pain.

Sung

          G5   B♭   C   B♭
Mother, father says things I've done I can't erase,
G5
Every night we fall from grace,
  B♭   C
Hard with the world in your face,
            E♭ F   G5
Try to hold on, try to hold on.

Chorus 3

G5   B♭   F
Faith, you know you're gonna live through the rain,
C   G5
Lord we've gotta keep the faith.
      B♭   F
Faith, don't you let your love turn to hate,
C   G5
Now we've gotta keep the faith,
       B♭   F
Keep the faith, keep the faith,
       E♭   F
Try to hold on, try to hold on.

Repeat to fade

CAN'T STAND LOSING YOU

Words and Music by Sting

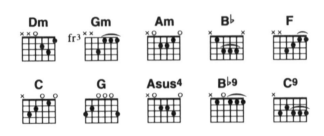

Intro | Dm Gm | Dm Gm | Dm Gm | Dm Gm ||

Verse 1

Dm   Am   Gm
Called you so many times today
      Dm   Am   Gm
And I guess it's all true what your girl friends say,
      Dm   Am   Gm
That you don't ever want so see me again,
         Dm   Am   Gm
And your brother's gonna kill me and he's six foot ten,

     B♭   F   B♭   F
I guess you'd call it cowardice
           C   G   C   Asus4
But I'm not prepared to go on like this.

Chorus 1

     B♭
I can't, I can't, I can't stand losing,
    Gm
I can't, I can't, I can't stand losing,
Asus4   Dm   Gm
I can't, I can't, I can't, I can't stand losing you,
Dm   Gm   Dm   Gm
   I can't stand losing you,
Dm Gm   Dm   Gm
   I can't stand losing you,
Dm   Gm   Dm   Gm   Dm Gm
   I can't stand losing you.

Verse 2

     Dm   **Am**   **Gm**
I see you've sent my letters back,

          Dm Am   **Gm**
And my L.P. records and they're all scratched.

     Dm   **Am**   **Gm**
I can't see the point in another day,

        Dm   **Am**   **Gm**
When nobody listens to a word I say.

        B♭   **F**   **B♭**   **F**
You can call it lack of confidence

        C   **G**   **C**   **Asus4**
But to carry on living doesn't make no sense.

Chorus 2

     B♭
I can't, I can't, I can't stand losing,

     Gm
I can't, I can't, I can't stand losing,

     Asus4
I can't, I can't, I can't stand losing,

     B♭
I can't, I can't, I can't stand losing,

     Gm
I can't, I can't, I can't stand losing,

     Asus4
I can't, I can't, I can't stand losing.

Instrumental ‖: **B♭9** | **B♭9** | **C9** | **C9** :‖

Middle

     Dm
I guess this is our last goodbye,

And you don't care so I won't cry,

And you'll be sorry when I'm dead

And all this guilt will blow your head.

   B♭   **F**   **B♭** **F**
I guess you'd call it suicide

     C   **G**   **C**   **Asus4**
But I'm too full to swallow my pride.

Chorus 3

B♭
I can't, I can't, I can't stand losing,

Gm
I can't, I can't, I can't stand losing,

Asus⁴
I can't, I can't, I can't stand losing,

B♭
I can't, I can't, I can't stand losing,

Gm
I can't, I can't, I can't stand losing,

Asus⁴
I can't, I can't, I can't stand losing,

Outro

‖:   **C**
I can't, I can't, I can't stand losing,

Asus⁴
I can't, I can't, I can't stand losing,

B♭
I can't, I can't, I can't stand losing. :‖   *Repeat to fade*

ROXANNE

Words and Music by Sting

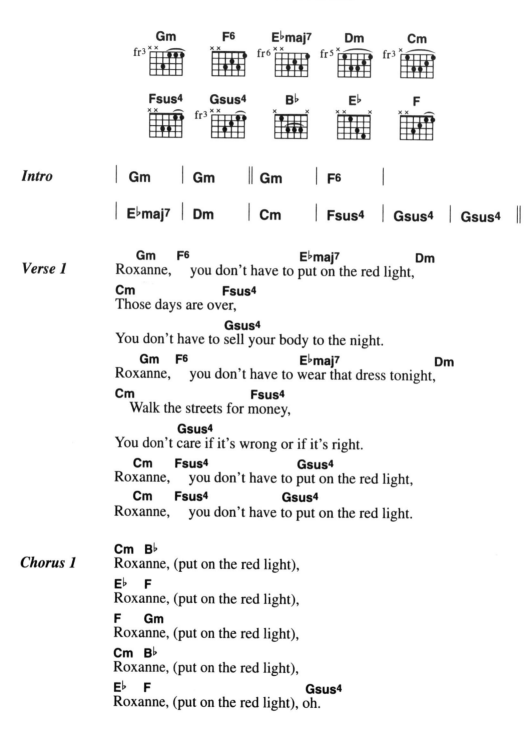

Intro

| Gm | Gm ‖ Gm | F6 |

| E♭maj7 | Dm | Cm | Fsus4 | Gsus4 | Gsus4 ‖

Verse 1

Gm   F6   E♭maj7   Dm
Roxanne,   you don't have to put on the red light,

Cm   Fsus4
Those days are over,

                 Gsus4
You don't have to sell your body to the night.

      Gm F6   E♭maj7   Dm
Roxanne,   you don't have to wear that dress tonight,

Cm   Fsus4
  Walk the streets for money,

          Gsus4
You don't care if it's wrong or if it's right.

    Cm Fsus4   Gsus4
Roxanne,   you don't have to put on the red light,

    Cm Fsus4   Gsus4
Roxanne,   you don't have to put on the red light.

Chorus 1

Cm B♭
Roxanne, (put on the red light),

E♭   F
Roxanne, (put on the red light),

F   Gm
Roxanne, (put on the red light),

Cm B♭
Roxanne, (put on the red light),

E♭   F   Gsus4
Roxanne, (put on the red light), oh.

Instrumental | Gm | Gm | Gm | Gm   ‖

.   Gm   F6
Verse 2   I loved you since I knew ya,

.   E♭maj7   Dm
.   I wouldn't talk down to ya,

.   Cm   Fsus4
.   I have to tell you just how I feel,

.   Gsus4
.   I won't share you with another boy.

.   Gm   F6
.   I know my mind is made up,

.   E♭maj7   Dm
.   So put away your make up,

.   Cm   Fsus4
.   Told you once, I won't tell you again,

.   Gsus4
.   It's a crime the way...

.   Cm   Fsus4   Gsus4
.   Roxanne,   you don't have to put on the red light,

.   Cm   Fsus4   Gsus4
.   Roxanne,   you don't have to put on the red light.

.   Cm B♭
Chorus 2   ‖: Roxanne, (put on the red light),

.   E♭   F
.   Roxanne, (put on the red light),

.   F   Gm
.   Roxanne, (put on the red light),

.   Cm B♭
.   Roxanne, (put on the red light).   :‖   *Repeat to fade*

SO LONELY

Words and Music by Sting

C   G   Am   F   D   A   Bm

Verse 1

C   G   Am   F
Well someone told me yesterday

C   G   Am   F
That when you throw your love away

C   G   Am   F
You act as if you just don't care,

C   G   Am   F
You look as if you're going somewhere.

C   G   Am   F
But I just can't convince myself,

C   G   Am   F
I couldn't live with no-one else,

C   G   Am   F
And I can only play that part

C   G   Am   F
And sit and nurse my broken heart.

Chorus 1

C   G   Am   F
So lonely, so lonely, so lonely,

C   G   Am   F
So lonely, so lonely, so lonely,

C   G   Am   F
So lonely, so lonely, so lonely,

C   G   Am   F
So lonely, so lonely, so lonely.

Verse 2

```
    C        G              Am        F
    Now no-one's knocked upon my door
    C    G        Am          F
    For a thousand years or more.
    C      G         Am        F
    All made up and nowhere to go,
    C    G          Am         F
    Welcome to this one-man show.
    C       G              Am        F
    Just take a seat, they're always free,
    C    G          Am     F
    No surprise, no mystery.
    C        G          Am         F
    In this theatre that I call my soul,
    C     G          Am          F
    I always play the starring role.
```

Chorus 2

```
    C          G           Am           F
    So lonely,  so lonely,  so lonely,
    C          G           Am           F
    So lonely,  so lonely,  so lonely,
    C          G           Am           F
    So lonely,  so lonely,  so lonely,
    C          G           Am           F
    So lonely,  so lonely,  so lonely.
```

Instrumental   ‖: D | A | Bm | G   :‖ *Play 7 times*

```
              | D    | A    | Bm    | G        ‖
                                       So lonely,
```

Outro   ‖: D   A   Bm   G
```
           so lonely,  so lonely,  so lonely.        :‖  Repeat to fade
```

GIRLS AND BOYS

Words and Music by Damon Albarn, Graham Coxon, Alex James and David Rowntree

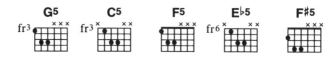

Verse 1

G5
Streets like a jungle,

C5
So call the police.

F5
Following the herd

           E♭5   **F♯5** **F5**
Down to Greece on holiday.

G5
Love in the nineties

C5
Is paranoid.

F5
On sunny beaches

           E♭5
Take your chances.

Chorus 1

F♯5   **F5**   **G5**
Looking for ‖: girls who are boys

Who like boys to be girls

           C5
Who do boys like they're girls

Who do girls like they're boys.

F5
Always should be someone

            E♭5   **F♯5** **F5**
You really love.   :‖

Instrumental   Chords as Chorus

Verse 2

G5
Avoiding all work

C5
'Cause there's none available.

F5
Like battery thinkers

E♭5   F♯5 F5
Count their thoughts on 1, 2, 3, 4, 5   fingers.

G5
Nothing is wasted,

C5
Only reproduced,

F5
You get nasty blisters.

E♭5
Du bist sehr schön

F♯5 F
But we haven't been introduced.

Chorus 2   ‖: G5
                    Girls who are boys who like boys

C5
To be girls who do boys

Like they're girls who do girls

Like they're boys.

F5
Always should be someone

E♭5   F♯5 F5
You really love.   :‖

Instrumental Chords as Chorus 2

Chorus 3   As Chorus 2

           Repeat to fade

165

PARKLIFE

Words and Music by Damon Albarn, Graham Coxon, Alex James and David Rowntree

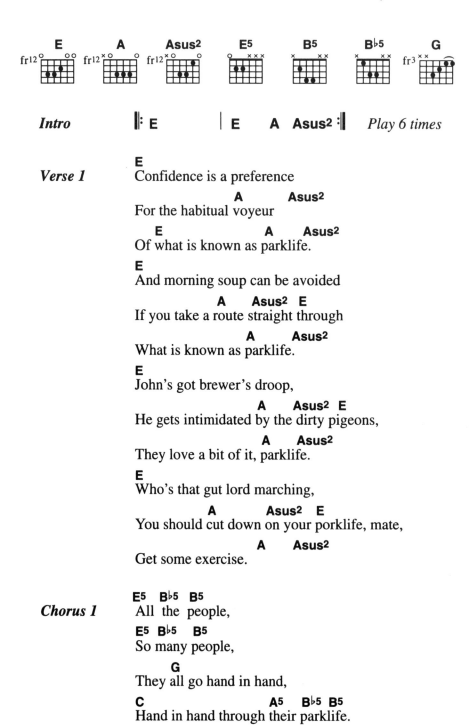

Intro   ‖: E | E   A   Asus2 :‖   *Play 6 times*

Verse 1
    E
Confidence is a preference
          A   **Asus2**
For the habitual voyeur
    E   **A**   **Asus2**
Of what is known as parklife.
  E
And morning soup can be avoided
         A   **Asus2** **E**
If you take a route straight through
           A   **Asus2**
What is known as parklife.
  E
John's got brewer's droop,
             A   **Asus2** **E**
He gets intimidated by the dirty pigeons,
          A   **Asus2**
They love a bit of it, parklife.
  E
Who's that gut lord marching,
         A   **Asus2** **E**
You should cut down on your porklife, mate,
            A   **Asus2**
Get some exercise.

Chorus 1
E5 **B♭5** **B5**
All the people,
E5 **B♭5**   **B5**
So many people,
     G
They all go hand in hand,
C   **A5** **B♭5** **B5**
Hand in hand through their parklife.

Instrumental | E | E   A Asus² | E | E   A E |

Verse 2

E
I get up when I want

              A
Except on Wednesday

        Asus² E   A   Asus²
When I get rudely awakened by the dustmen (parklife).

E
I put my trousers on,

            A   Asus²
Have a cup of tea

         E   A   Asus²
And I think about leaving the house (parklife).

E
I feed the pigeons,

            A   Asus²
I sometimes feed the sparrows too,

E   A   Asus²
It gives me a sense of enormous well-being (parklife),

E
And then I'm happy for the rest of the day,

A   Asus²   E
Safe in the knowledge that there will always be

                       A   Asus²
A bit of my heart devoted to it.

Chorus 2   As Chorus 1

E   A   Asus² E   A   Asus²
       Parklife,   (parklife),

E   A   Asus² E   A   Asus²
       Parklife,   (parklife).

E
It's got nothing to do with your

                    A   Asus²
Vorsprung durch technic, you know

E
And it's not about your joggers

                  A   Asus²
Who go round and round and round.

Chorus 3   As Chorus 1

           Repeat to fade

COUNTRY HOUSE

Words and Music by Damon Albarn, Graham Coxon, Alex James and David Rowntree

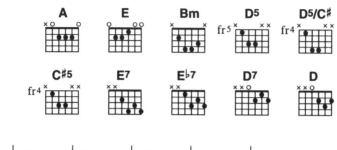

Intro | A | E | Bm | Bm |

| D5 | D5/C# | C#5 | C#5 |

Spoken   So the story begins.

Verse 1

A
City dweller,

   E
Successful feller,

Bm
Thought to himself, "Oops,

I've got a lot of money,

D5   D5/C#   C#5
Caught in a rat race terminally,

       A
I'm a professional cynic

      E
But my heart's not in it,

   Bm
I'm paying the price of living life at the limit,

D5   D5/C#   C#5
Caught up in the century's anxiety".

     E
Yes, it preys on him,

He's getting thin.

Chorus 1

    A   **E7**   **E♭7**   **D7**
Now he lives in a house, a very big house in the country,

Watching afternoon repeats
                                 A
And the food that he eats in the country.

He takes all manner of pills
                             E7   **E♭7** **D7**
And piles up analyst's bills in the country.

Ooh, it's like an Animal Farm,
                         A
Lots of rural charm in the country.

Verse 2

     A
He's got morning glory
   E
And life's a different story,
Bm
Everything's going Jackanory,
D5   **D5/C♯**   **C♯5**
In touch with his own mortality.
   A   **E**
He's reading Balzac, knocking back Prozac,
     Bm   **D5**
It's a helping hand that makes you feel wonderfully bland,
       D5/C♯   **C♯5**
Oh, it's the century's remedy
      E
For the faint of heart, a new start.

Chorus 2

     A   **E7**   **E♭7**   **D7**
He lives in a house, a very big house in the country,

He's got a frog in his chest
                              A
So he needs a lot of rest in the country.

He doesn't drink, smoke, laugh,
                      E7   **E♭7**   **D7**
Takes herbal baths in the country,

But you'll come to no harm
                         A
On the Animal Farm in the country.

E
In the country,

In the country,

In the country.

Instrumental   Chords as Verse

Bridge

A   **E**
Blow, blow me out
        D
I am so sad,
            A
I don't know why.
A   **E**
Blow, blow me out
        D
I am so sad,
            A
I don't know why.

Chorus 3   As Chorus 1

Chorus 4   As Chorus 2

Instrumental   Chords as Chorus   *Repeat to fade*

REMEMBER HOW WE STARTED

Words and Music by Paul Weller

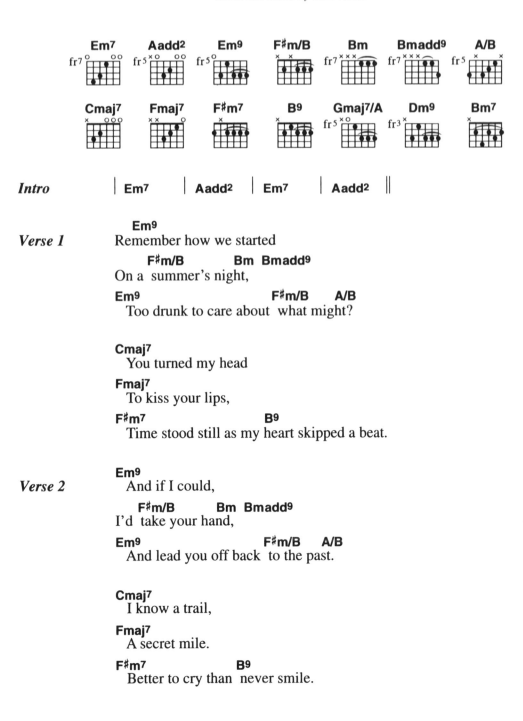

Intro

| Em7 | Aadd2 | Em7 | Aadd2 ‖

Verse 1

    Em9
Remember how we started

    F♯m/B   **Bm Bmadd9**
On a summer's night,

Em9   **F♯m/B**   **A/B**
  Too drunk to care about what might?

Cmaj7
  You turned my head

Fmaj7
  To kiss your lips,

F♯m7   **B9**
  Time stood still as my heart skipped a beat.

Verse 2

Em9
  And if I could,

    F♯m/B   **Bm Bmadd9**
I'd take your hand,

Em9   **F♯m/B**   **A/B**
  And lead you off back to the past.

Cmaj7
  I know a trail,

Fmaj7
  A secret mile.

F♯m7   **B9**
  Better to cry than never smile.

| **Em7** | **Aadd2** | **Em7** | **Aadd2** ||

Verse 3

Em9
The moonlight shining

          F#m/B   **Bm Bmadd9**
Through your flowered curtains,

Em9   **F#m/B**   **A/B**
I think we knew it was us for certain.

Cmaj7
And just the thing

Fmaj7
That we hoped for,

F#m7   **B9**
Was building up into something more.

Bridge 1

Gmaj7/A   **Dm9**
Oh I've been searching, searching,

Gmaj7/A   **Dm9**
Trying to find the words to say.

Gmaj7/A   **Dm9**
Oh, I've been searching, searching,

Gmaj7/A   **Cmaj7**   **Bm7**   **Em9**
Trying to get back to the love we made yesterday.

Sax solo ||: **Em9** | **F#m/B A/B** | **Em9** | **F#m/B A/B** :||

Em7   **Aadd2**
Oh, I think we'll find a way,

Em7 Aadd2
I   think we'll find a way.

Verse 4

    Em9
Remember how we started

      F#m/B   **Bm Bmadd9**
On a summer's night?

Em9   **F#m/B**
Too young to know about what might.

Cmaj7
Just as well,

Fmaj7
As we might not

F#m7   **B9**
Of ever started on this course at all.

Outro

Em9
Remember how we started

   F#m/B
On a summer's night?

   Em9   F#m/B
Remember how we started?

   Em9
Remember how we started

   F#m/B
On a summer's night?

   Em9   F#m/B
Remember how we started?

Em9 F#m/B Em9 F#m/B
             I think we'll find a way,

Em9   F#m/B   Em9 F#m/B
  Oh, I think we'll find a way, yeah.

FOOT OF THE MOUNTAIN

Words and Music by Paul Weller

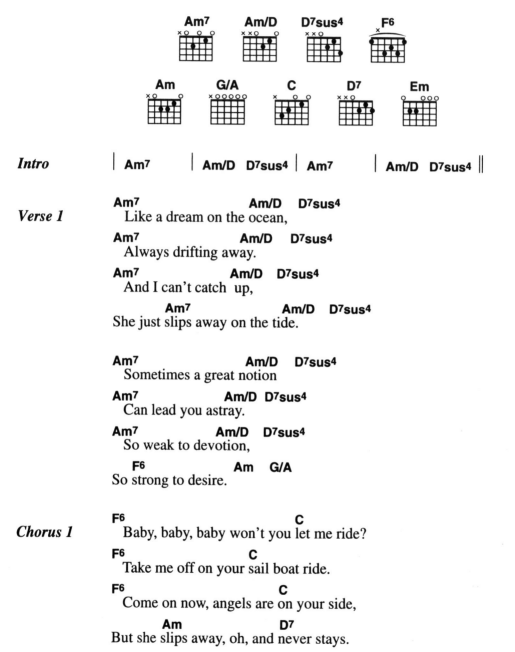

Intro
| Am7 | Am/D D7sus4 | Am7 | Am/D D7sus4 ||

Verse 1

Am7　　　　　　　　Am/D　D7sus4
　Like a dream on the ocean,

Am7　　　　　　　　Am/D　D7sus4
　Always drifting away.

Am7　　　　　　Am/D　D7sus4
　And I can't catch up,

　　　Am7　　　　　Am/D　D7sus4
She just slips away on the tide.

Am7　　　　　　　　　Am/D　D7sus4
　Sometimes a great notion

Am7　　　　　　Am/D　D7sus4
　Can lead you astray.

Am7　　　　　Am/D　D7sus4
　So weak to devotion,

　F6　　　　　　　Am　G/A
So strong to desire.

Chorus 1

F6　　　　　　　　　　　C
　Baby, baby, baby won't you let me ride?

F6　　　　　　　C
　Take me off on your sail boat ride.

F6　　　　　　　　　　C
　Come on now, angels are on your side,

　　Am　　　　　　D7
But she slips away, oh, and never stays.

Instrumental | Am7 | Am/D D7sus4 | Am7 | Am/D D7sus4 |

| Am7 | Am/D D7sus4 | Am7 | Am7 ||

Verse 2

Am7   Am/D   D7sus4
   Like mercury gliding,

Am7   Am/D   D7sus4
  A silver teardrop that falls.

Am7   Am/D   D7sus4
  And I can't hold on,

         Am7   Am/D   D7sus4
Through my fingers she's gone.

Am7   Am/D   D7sus4
  At the foot of the mountain,

Am7   Am/D   D7sus4
  Such a long way to climb.

Am7   Am/D   D7sus4
  How will I ever get up there?

   F6   Am   G/A
But know I must try.

Chorus 2

F6   C
  Baby, baby, baby won't you let me ride?

F6   C
  Take me off on your sail boat ride.

F6   C
  Come on now, angels are on your side,

      Am   D7   Am7 D7sus4
But she slips away, oh, and never stays.

Verse 3

Am7   Am/D   D7sus4
  Like a dream on the ocean,

Am7   Am/D   D7sus4
  Always drifting away.

Am7   Am/D
  And I can't catch up,

     Am7   Am/D
She just slips away.

   Am7   D7
Oh, slips away,

   Am7   D7 Em Am7
Oh, slips away.

HOW DO YOU SLEEP

Words and Music by John Squire

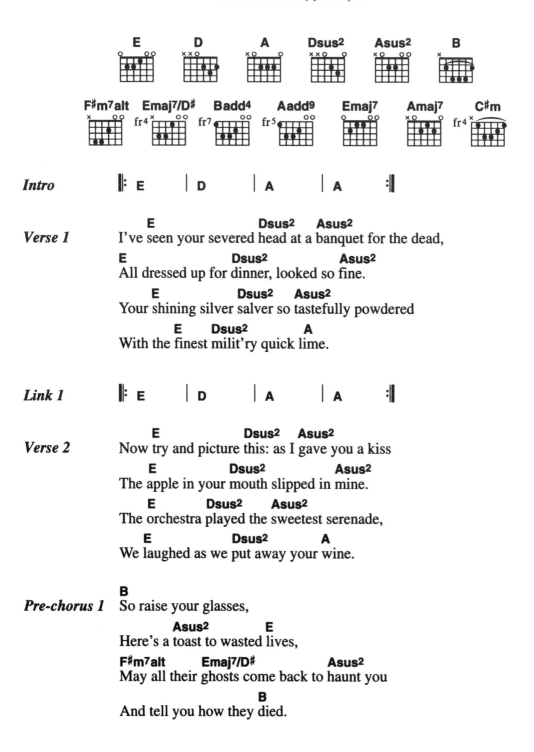

Intro

‖: E | D | A | A :‖

Verse 1

E   Dsus2   Asus2
I've seen your severed head at a banquet for the dead,

E   Dsus2   Asus2
All dressed up for dinner, looked so fine.

E   Dsus2   Asus2
Your shining silver salver so tastefully powdered

E   Dsus2   A
With the finest milit'ry quick lime.

Link 1

‖: E | D | A | A :‖

Verse 2

E   Dsus2   Asus2
Now try and picture this: as I gave you a kiss

E   Dsus2   Asus2
The apple in your mouth slipped in mine.

E   Dsus2   Asus2
The orchestra played the sweetest serenade,

E   Dsus2   A
We laughed as we put away your wine.

Pre-chorus 1

B
So raise your glasses,

Asus2   E
Here's a toast to wasted lives,

F#m7alt   Emaj7/D#   Asus2
May all their ghosts come back to haunt you

B
And tell you how they died.

Chorus 1

(B)   E   Badd⁴   Aadd⁹   Badd⁴

How do you sleep, how do you last the night and keep the dogs at bay?

               E   Badd⁴   Aadd⁹   Badd⁴

How do you feel when you close your eyes and try to drift away?

        Emaj⁷   F♯m⁷alt   Emaj⁷/D♯ F♯m⁷alt

Does it feel any better now, does it mean any more?

            E   F♯m⁷alt   Amaj⁷

When the angel of death comes knock, knocking

     B   E

And banging at your door?

Link 2   ‖: E | D | A | A   :‖

Verse 3

           E   Dsus² Asus²

When all the fun was over, I put you on my shoulder,

E   Dsus²   Asus²

Took you home away from it all.

E   Dsus²   Asus²

Shot down and claimed, mounted and framed,

E   Dsus²   A

Tastefully hung up on my wall.

Pre-chorus 2

         B

Are my dreams your nightmares?

   Asus²   E

I hope they all come true.

F♯m⁷alt   Emaj⁷/D♯   Asus²

Get off your knees, the party's over,

                 B

I'm coming home to you.

Chorus 2   As Chorus 1

Guitar solo | E | B | Asus² | E | F♯m⁷alt | Emaj⁷/D♯ |

           | Aadd⁹ | Aadd⁹ | Badd⁴ | Badd⁴ ‖

Chorus 3   As Chorus 1

Coda | D | C♯m | B | E   ‖

        At your door.

I WANNA BE ADORED

Words and Music by Ian Brown and John Squire

G   D   Em   C

Intro   ‖: G   D | G   D | Em | Em :‖ *Play 8 times*

Verse 1

G D   G D   Em
I don't have to sell my soul,

He's already in me.

G D   G D   Em
I don't need to sell my soul,

He's already in me.

Chorus 1

G D G   D Em
     I wanna be adored,

G D G   D Em
     I wanna be adored.

Instrumental | G   D | G   D | Em | Em ‖

Verse 2

G D   G D   Em
I don't need to sell my soul,

He's already in me.

G D   G D   Em
I don't have to sell my soul,

He's already in me.

Chorus 2

G D G   D Em
     I wanna be adored,

G D G   D Em
     I wanna be adored.

Solo ‖: D   C | D   C | D   C | D   C :‖

| D | D   ‖

       | G D | G D | Em |
Chorus 3   A - dor - - - - - - - - ed,

       G D G   D   Em
          I wanna be adored.

         G   D G D   Em
Coda   You adore me,   you adore me,

           G
         You adore me.

         D   G   D   Em
       I wanna, I wanna, I wanna be adored.
                                    G
       I wanna, I wanna, I wanna be adored.
         D   G   D   Em
       I wanna, I wanna, I wanna be adored.
                               G   D | G D | Em | Em |
       I wanna, I wanna, I gotta be adored.

       | G D | G D | Em | Em |

       G D G   D   Em
          I wanna be adored.

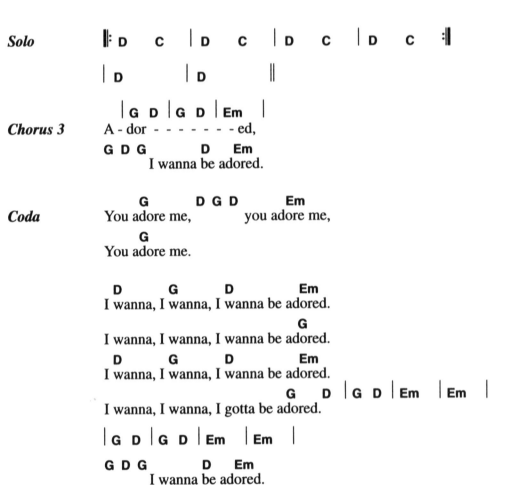

WATERFALL

Words and Music by Ian Brown and John Squire

F#   F#sus4   B   Bmaj7   G#m

C#   C#7sus4   C#m7   E   Emaj7

Intro

| F#   F#sus4 | F#   F#sus4 | F#   F#sus4 | F#   F#sus4 ‖

Verse 1

F#   F#sus4   F#   F#sus4
Chimes sing Sunday morn,____

   F#   F#sus4   F#   F#sus4
Today's __ the day she's sworn __

   B   Bmaj7   G#m
To steal what she never could own

   B   Bmaj7   C#   C#7sus4 | F#   F#sus4 | F#   F#sus4 ‖
And race from this hole she calls home.

Verse 2

F#   F#sus4   F#   F#sus4
Now __ you're at the wheel,____

    F#   F#sus4   F#   F#sus4
Tell me how, __ how does it feel? ___

   B   Bmaj7   G#m
So good to have equal - ised,

   B   Bmaj7   C#   C#7sus4 | F#   F#sus4 | F#   F#sus4 ‖
To lift up the lids of your eyes.

Verse 3

    F#   F#sus4   F#   F#sus4
As the miles __ they disappear,____

  F#   F#sus4   F#   F#sus4
See land __ begin to clear __

  B   Bmaj7   G#m
Free from filth and the scum.

   B   Bmaj7   C#   C#7sus4 | F#   F#sus4 | F#   F#sus4 ‖
This American satellite's won.

Chorus 1

E   Emaj7   C#m7
She'll carry on through it all,

              F# F#sus4 | F# F#sus4 |
She's a waterfall.

E   Emaj7   C#m7 C#7sus4
She'll carry on through it all,

              F# F#sus4 | F# F#sus4 ‖
She's a waterfall.

Verse 4

F# F#sus4   F#   F#sus4
See __ the steeple pine, ____

    F#   F#sus4   F#   F#sus4
The hills __ as old as time, __

B   Bmaj7   G#m
Soon to be put to the test,

    B   Bmaj7   C# C#7sus4 | F# F#sus4 | F# F#sus4 ‖
To be whipped by the winds of the west.

Verse 5

F#   F#sus4   F#   F#sus4
Stands __ on shifting sands, ____

    F#   F#sus4   F#   F#sus4
The scales __ held in her hands. __

B   Bmaj7   G#m
The wind it just whips her and wails

    B   Bmaj7   C# C#7sus4 | F# F#sus4 | F# F#sus4 ‖
And fills up her brigantine sails.

Chorus 2   As Chorus 1

Outro

| G#m | B | G#m | B C# |

‖: F# | F# | F# | F# :‖ *Ad lib. to fade*

181

4 A.M.

Words and Music by Simon Friend, Charles Heather, Mark Chadwick, Jonathon Sevink and Jeremy Cunningham

[chord diagrams: G*, Am*, C, F5, F/E, G5, G, F, F/A, Am]

Intro   ‖: G* Am* G* Am* G* C | C | G F5 | F/E F F/E F G5 :‖

Verse 1

Am   C   G   F
It's four o'clock in the morning, we're still putting the world to rights,

Am   C G   F
The whiskey's started talking, there's a fire in your eyes.

G   Am
Conspiracy lies heavy in ev'ry word you breathe,

G   Am
Contentious bones, widely known, watering the seeds.

Chorus 1

F   C
Be sure to send a postcard,

G   Am
When you get there let me know,

F   C   G
You know that I won't stop you when you go.

Inst. 1   ‖: Am   C | C | G   F | F :‖

Verse 2

Am   C   G F
It's five o'clock in the morning and you're glad to be alive,

Am   C   G   F
The booze has finished working, the world is on your side.

G   Am
It's clear to see the tyranny was all some kind of plot,

G   Am
You secretly confide in me, where there's brass, there's muck.

Chorus 2   As Chorus 1

Chorus 3

```
       F                C
Be sure to send a postcard,
           G              Am
When you get there let me know,
       F              C           G
I hope that you can make it on your own.
```

```
‖: G* Am* G* Am* | G* Am* G* Am* | G* Am* G* Am* | C  G      :‖

‖: Am    C | C           | G       F | F         G :‖   Play 4 times
```

Verse 3

```
        Am                                    C    G    F
It's six o'clock in the morning and there's nowhere left to hide,
Am                          C   G      F
Now we've seen the dawn in, all that's left is our goodbyes.
       G                 Am
It's hard to see the sanity in what we call our lives,
G                               Am
Sometimes it seems that you just need to follow what's inside.
```

Chorus 4

```
       F                C
Be sure to send a postcard,
           G              Am
When you get there let me know,
       F              C           G
You know that I won't stop you when you go.
```

Chorus 5

```
       F                C
Be sure to send a postcard,
           G              Am
When you get there let me know,
       F              C         G
I hope that you will make it all alone.
```

Chorus 6

```
       F                C
Be sure to send a postcard,
           G              Am
When you get there let me know,
       F              C           G
I hope that you can make it on your own.
```

ANIMAL NITRATE

Words and Music by Brett Anderson and Bernard Butler

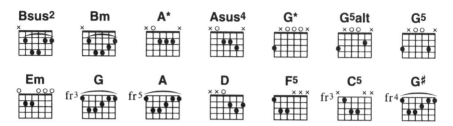

Tune guitar down one semitone

Intro

| Bsus2 Bm Bsus2 A* Asus4 A* | G* G5alt G5 Em | |

‖: Bm   A* Asus4 A* | G   Em :‖   *Play 3 times*

Verse 1

      Bm A   G   Em
Like his   dad you know that he's had
Bm   A   G   Em
Animal nitrate in mind.
          Bm   A   G   Em
Oh, in your council home he jumped on your bones,
          Bm   A   G
Now you're taking it time after time.

Chorus 1

        A   D G D G
Oh, it turns you on, ___ on, ___
Bm   A   G
And now he has gone.
        A   D G D G
Oh, what turns you on, ___ on, ___
Bm   A   F5   C5
Now your animal's gone? ___

Verse 1

      Bm A   G   Em
Well he   said he'd show you his bed
          Bm   A   G   Em
And the delights of the chemical smile, ___
          Bm   A   G   Em
So in your broken home he broke all your bones,
          Bm   A   G
Now you're taking it time after time.

Chorus 2

       A   **D** **G** **D** **G**
Oh, it turns you on, ___ on, ___

Bm   **A**   **G**
And now he has gone.

          A   **D** **G** **D** **G**
Oh, what turns you on, ___ on, ___

Bm   **A**   **F5**   **C5**
Now your animal's gone? ___

Solo

| **Bm** **G** | **G#** **G** | **Bm** **G** | **G#** **G** |

| **Bm** **G** | **G#** **G** | **Bm** **G** | **G#** **G** ‖

Chorus 3

A   **D** **G** **D** **G**
  What does it take to turn you on, ___ on, ___

Bm **A**   **G**
  Now he has gone?

               A   **D** **G** **D** **G**
Now you're over twenty one? ___ Oh, ___

Bm   **A**   **G**
Now your animal's gone?

Outro

   (G) **D**   **G**   **D** **G**
‖: Animal, he was animal, ___

       Bm **A** **G**
An animal, ___ oh. :‖   *Repeat to fade with vocal ad lib.*

STILL LIFE

Words and Music by Brett Anderson and Bernard Butler

Dsus2	Dsus4	D	G	Em

B♭maj7	A7	A	F6	B♭	Gm

Tune guitar down one semitone

Intro

| Dsus2 | Dsus4 D | G | G | |
| Em | B♭maj7 A7 | A7 | A7 | ‖ |

Verse 1

    Dsus2 **Dsus4** **D**
This still   life _____

  G
Is all I ever do,

Em   **B♭maj7**   **A**   **Dsus4** **D**
There by the window quietly killed for you.

    Dsus2 **Dsus4** **D**
In this glass   house_____

   G
My insect life

Em   **B♭maj7**   **A**   **D**
Crawling the walls under electric lights.

    F6   **Em**
I'll go into the night,

      A7
Into the night,

F6   **Em**
She and I _____

      A7
Into the night.

Verse 2

        Dsus² Dsus⁴ D
Is this still   life ____

G
All I'm good for too?

Em   **B♭maj⁷**   **A**   **Dsus⁴ D**
There by the window quietly killed for you.

        Dsus² Dsus⁴ D
And they drive   by ____

    G
Like insects do,

    Em
They think they don't know me,

    B♭maj⁷   **A**   **D**
They hired a car for you.

      F⁶   **Em**
To go into the night,

      A⁷
Into the night,

F⁶   **Em**
She and I ____

      A⁷
Into the night.

Verse 3

      Dsus² Dsus⁴ D
And this   still life ____

   G
Is all I ever do,

Em   **B♭maj⁷**   **A**   **Dsus⁴ D**
There by the window quietly killed for you.

      Dsus²   **G**
And this still life is all I ever do,

      Em B♭ **A** **D** **A⁷**
But it's still, still ____ life,

      D   **G**   **Gm**
But it's still, still life,

      Em **A**   **Dsus²** **D** **Dsus²** **D** **A⁷**
But it's still, still life.

Instrumental

Dsus²	D	G	G	Em	B♭ A
D	A⁷	Dsus²	D	G	G
Em	A⁷	D	A	A	A
Dsus²	Dsus²	Dsus²	Dsus²	Dsus²	Dsus²	D ‖

BEAUTIFUL ONES

Words and Music by Brett Anderson and Richard Oakes

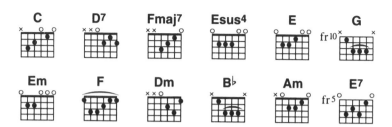

Tune guitar down one semitone

Intro
‖: C | D7 | Fmaj7 | Esus4 E :‖

Verse 1
         C   D7
Ooh, high on diesel and gasoline,

           Fmaj7
Psycho for drum machine,

              Esus4   E
Shaking their bits to the hits, oh.

C   D7
Drag acts, drug acts, suicides,

           Fmaj7
In your dad's suit you hide,

           Esus4 E
Staining his name again, oh.

Verse 2
      C   D7
Cracked up, stacked up, twenty-two,

           Fmaj7
Psycho for sex and glue,

         Esus4 E
Lost it in Bostik, yeah.

        C   D7
Oh, shaved heads, rave heads, on the pill,

         Fmaj7
Got too much time to kill,

        E   G
Get into the bands and gangs, oh.

Chorus 1

C
Here they come,

    Em
The beautiful ones,

    F
The beautiful ones,

Dm   B♭
La la la la.

C
Here they come,

    Em
The beautiful ones,

    F
The beautiful ones,

Dm   B♭   Am E7
La la la la la,   la la.

Verse 3

C   D7
Loved up, doved up, hung around,

            Fmaj7
Stoned in a lonely town,

             Esus4   E
Shaking their meat to the beat, oh.

C   D7
High on diesel and gasoline,

            Fmaj7
Psycho for drum machine,

             Esus4   E   G
Shaking their bits to the hits, oh.

Chorus 2

C
Here they come,

    Em
The beautiful ones,

    F
The beautiful ones,

Dm   B♭
La la la la.

C
Here they come,

    Em
The beautiful ones,

    F   Dm
The beautiful ones, oh oh.

Bridge

B♭   **C**
You don't think about it,

         Em
You don't do without it,

        F   **Dm**
Because you're beautiful, yeah, yeah.

B♭   **C**   **Em**
  And if your baby's going crazy,

        F   **Dm**
That's how you made me, la la.

B♭   **C**   **Em**
  And if your baby's going crazy,

        F   **Dm**
That's how you made me, woah woah,

B♭   **C**   **Em**
  And if your baby's going crazy,

        F
That's how you made me,

Dm **B♭** **Am** **E7**
La la, la la, la. La, la.

Outro

‖: **C**   **D7**
La la la la, la,

        Fmaj7
La la la la la, la.

         Esus4
La la la la la la,

   E
La la la, oh. :‖ *Repeat to fade*